ZAMANI THOMAS

THE CREATIVE SHIELD

THE ARTIST'S GUIDE TO COPYRIGHTS, TRADEMARKS & BRAND MONETIZATION

The: Creative-Docket
Toronto - Miami

The Creative Docket

The Creative Shield

The Artist's Guide to Copyrights, Trademarks & Brand Monetization

Volume I in The Creative Shield Series

Published by: The Creative Docket Toronto, Canada www.thecreativedocket.com

ISBN: 978-1-0694144-4-1 Printed in the United States of America

Editor: Brandi Sousa

Cover design and artwork: Imhotep Design and Zamani Thomas

10 9 8 7 6 5 4 3 2 1 First Edition

The Creative Shield

Your Legal Toolkit for the Digital Age

You create with passion. Protect it with knowledge.

The Creative Shield Series is a 3-part guide for artists and creative entrepreneurs who want to understand their rights, protect their work, and move with confidence into the future of art in the age of AI.

Volume I - Copyrights, Trademarks & Brand Monetization

Lay a solid foundation. Master the legal mechanisms to assert and protect your creations, cultivate a distinct brand, and confidently embrace your artistic identity.

Volume II - Contracts, Licensing & Revenue Streams *(Coming 2025)*

Transform your art into revenue, on your terms. This volume dissects agreements, contracts, royalties, and licensing, empowering you to expand your business while retaining control over your creations.

Volume III - AI, Digital Protection & Emerging Tech *(Coming Soon)*

The future is now. From AI innovations to NFTs and beyond, this volume equips you to navigate emerging technologies, comprehend your rights in the digital realm, and preserve your artistic legacy in a continually evolving environment.

This series serves as your protective gear. It is practical, empowering, and designed to help you secure what you create, earn what you deserve, and establish a lasting legacy.

Create it. Own it. Share it.

Contents

Contracts

Infringement

Digital IP

Legacy

Legend

● Case Study

Real-world examples illustrating key IP law and brand lessons.

■ Artist Example

Real-world case or creative strategy.

>> Artist Takeaway

Insight or lesson from a legal issue.

** Artist Tip

Practical advice for artists.

▣ QR Code

Scan to download templates and tools.

Toolkit

Templates, checklists, and charts. Full-color visuals are available online.

Toolkit Page

Can't scan a QR code? No problem.
Find everything at: thecreativedocket.com/toolkit.

Preface

For more than two decades, I have been working at the intersection of art and law, assisting artists from all disciplines and major corporations with navigating the intricate world of intellectual property law. I've witnessed firsthand how a simple idea or spark can transform an artist from a relative unknown into a superstar. I've also frequently observed the consequences of artists neglecting their asset protection strategies. Whether representing Fortune 500 companies, managing intellectual property portfolios for celebrity clients, or advising well-established and recognizable brands, one truth remains the same: **Ownership Matters.**

The Creative Shield's fundamental mission is to empower artists, creative professionals, and entrepreneurs of all levels to take ownership of their work while safeguarding their intellectual property. Although this book is primarily tailored to artists, its principles apply to anyone looking to protect their brand, work, and legacy in this ever-evolving, interconnected digital world.

I've encountered many talented artists and innovators who believe that legal protections are the domain of large corporations or established brands. The truth is that intellectual property assets—whether copyrights, trademarks, or patents—are not strictly the province of large companies; they also form the foundation upon which emerging artists and small businesses can build lasting success. Unfortunately, it's all too common for artists to seek legal counsel only after their intellectual property has been jeopardized through the exploitation or theft of their work. Once this occurs, the damage to their brand is often too significant to recover from.

The purpose of this book is to change that narrative and allow artists to flourish without the burden of legal peril. This is not a legal text but a practical guide created to equip creatives with the knowledge and strategies needed to safeguard their work at the outset of the creative process. Within these pages, you will find insights on trademarks and copyrights, strategies for licensing, digital protection, and other emerging challenges posed by technologies such as artificial intelligence and blockchain. My goal is to ensure that you understand and feel confident in asserting your rights.

Artists who consider legal matters an afterthought or only an issue for the corporate world must adopt a different mindset and implement the strategies presented in this book. Owning your intellectual property means securing your future. Your creations are yours, and you should be able to dictate how they are used while being compensated fairly.

Once you've transformed a unique idea into a valuable creation, the hard part is done. Now, let's make sure it remains yours.

Creativity extends beyond mere inspiration; it is a potent force that can be harnessed. We inhabit a fast-paced world where ideas proliferate rapidly, with artificial intelligence and social media blurring the boundaries between originality and imitation. As a creator, it is vital to safeguard your unique work. This book serves as both your defensive strategy and your guide; it aims to empower you to protect, monetize, and cultivate a resilient brand. If you are ready to transform your vision into a secure and profitable reality, let's get started.

Note To Artists

The insights in this book are designed to support artists from all walks of life, but it is important to note that the legal frameworks discussed are primarily focused on U.S. intellectual property law. If you're creating outside of the United States, be sure to connect with a legal professional in your country to ensure you're protecting your work according to your local laws.

Also, as a reminder, as you scan through these pages, the creative and legal landscape is constantly evolving. Court rulings shift, common law develops, and cultural norms continue to reshape how we think about ownership, originality, and value. Some of what you'll read here may change with time, and that's okay.

This book is a living conversation meant to grow with you. Use it as a compass, not a cage. Return to it when you need clarity, direction, or a reminder that your work is worth protecting. Now, let's step into the world of creative ownership, together.

All charts, templates, and full-color visuals referenced in this book are available *at* thecreativedocket.com/toolkit. If a QR code isn't working, that link provides direct access.

Branding

Crafting Your Name

1.1 Understanding Branding

What is a Brand

A brand transcends mere logos and slogans; it serves as a true representation of your identity! It encapsulates how others perceive you and your business, resonating with the values and emotions you yearn to express. Whether portraying a company, a passion project, or another venture, a brand serves as a vital link between the creator and the audience.

For artists, this identity connection is profoundly valued. Your brand embodies your fundamental beliefs and essence. While artists champion creativity and uniqueness, nonprofits embody compassion and hope. Although these entities may share similar ideals, their priorities can vary widely. At the core of branding lies the art of creating an unforgettable identity that resonates deeply with your audience.

This focus on identity strengthens your emotional bond with your audience through your work or name. When your audience connects with your narrative rather than simply your products, you evolve from just another name into a resonant brand (Holt, 2004).

Understanding what a brand is builds the foundation; now, let's explore why branding matters so much for creative professionals.

Why Brands Matter

Consider icons like Banksy, Kehinde Wiley, or Erykah Badu. They embody more than talent; they evoke intense feelings tied to significant cultural experiences: a mural that challenged societal norms, a portrait that reshaped representation, or a song that resonates with your innermost thoughts. These identities convey far beyond a name or aesthetic; they stir emotion, memory, and aspiration. Such influence arises from deliberate choices and the lasting impact these artists leave on their audience.

Artists often find more in common with traditional professionals than we might think, especially regarding brand development. A powerful brand cultivates trust and authority. It communicates consistency, which is essential for fostering loyalty. When your audience knows what to expect from you, they gain confidence in supporting your work. This trust forms the foundation for enduring relationships, repeat commissions, and the ability to charge what your work is worth, not just based on quality, but also on the value of your reputation (Godin, 2003).

Beyond being a business tool, your brand serves as a vehicle for personal empowerment. When you cultivate a brand that mirrors your vision, values, or artistic mission, you affirm your identity and define your creative journey. It positions you as a pioneer in your domain, opening doors to new possibilities and courageous steps in your career.

From a professional viewpoint, branding provides you with a competitive advantage. It distinguishes your work from others offering similar styles or services. Those emotional connections and moments of recognition are what render your brand unforgettable and your presence irreplaceable.

Standing Out

In today's crowded economy, differentiation isn't just about standing out; it's about standing for something. The artists who gain traction aren't necessarily the loudest; they're the ones who resonate. Your brand should clarify why you create, who it's for, and how you want your work to impact others.

This is especially powerful in niche markets. An artist who works exclusively with recycled materials, for example, can attract both art lovers and sustainability advocates. That's not just aesthetic, that's purpose-driven branding. When your values guide your message, your brand becomes more than memorable. It becomes meaningful.

Practically, this might mean building a cohesive visual identity, telling stories that reflect your artistic philosophy, or refining your social presence so that everything you share aligns with your intention. Distinction comes not from volume, but from clarity.

(For insights into how your brand identity translates into licensing opportunities and revenue, refer to 5.2 Licensing for Profit.)

Personal vs. Artistic

Your brand can be deeply personal without being your whole self. This gives you freedom to evolve, explore, and protect parts of your life that don't need to be public while still building a brand that feels honest and meaningful.

Now that we've covered identity and impact, let's turn to the intersection of creativity and commerce, and how brand strategy fuels career growth.

1.2 Creativity & Commerce

Business Savvy

Artists often immerse themselves in the purity of their craft, placing their creations at the center of their existence. Yet, in today's landscape, artistic achievement goes beyond mere talent; it demands a savvy grasp of the business domain.

Many artists fear that business will dilute their creativity, but the opposite is true. Viewing art through a business lens helps it thrive. Knowing your audience clarifies your goals and strategies, enhancing both visibility and revenue. This might mean creating exclusive pricing or using social media to share your process and boost accessibility.

Take the journey of Jean-Michel Basquiat, who transitioned from a street artist with a passionate following to a revered figure in the international art scene

(Green, 2019). While his natural talent initially sparked interest, it was the strategic guidance of art dealer Larry Gagosian and others that elevated his brand. Basquiat's narrative exemplifies how blending creativity with commercial awareness can amplify an artist's influence and legacy.

Artists hesitant about legal matters can still flourish by partnering with trusted advisors, agents, or managers, allowing them to focus on their artistry. Striving for commercial success doesn't overshadow creativity; rather, the right support enables artists to receive proper recognition and financial rewards.

Building a brand is one thing, protecting it is another. And both are essential to long-term success.

Protecting Brand Value

The art world is replete with tales of creators losing their rights due to inadequate protective measures. A well-defined brand serves as a safeguard, preserving your artistic essence and ensuring control over it.

From a financial perspective, safeguarding your identity fosters stability and opens pathways for growth. Consider musician Taylor Swift, who famously re-recorded her earlier albums to reclaim ownership of her master recordings (Hobbs, 2021). This bold action underscored the significance of ownership and illustrated how brand protection can unlock new revenue streams. Swift's reimagined music resonated with a new generation of fans, all while staying true to her artistic vision.

On the reputational front, brand protection provides substantial advantages. A cohesive, authentic, and legally fortified brand builds trust with your audience. Whether you are an artist selling prints or a chef introducing a new meal line, your brand's reputation becomes synonymous with excellence and dependability.

The streetwear company Supreme stands as a testament to this principle, achieving global notoriety through its trademarked logo and meticulously crafted identity (Wikipedia, 2024). The company diligently defends its intellectual property against imitations, ensuring its products maintain value through their uniqueness and quality. Actively safeguarding a brand enhances its worth and solidifies its place as a cultural and commercial leader.

Smaller examples further underline the necessity of brand protection. An independent jewelry designer, for instance, can shield their logo from competitors aiming to replicate their style (Lessig, 2004). As independent creators generally operate with narrower profit margins, protecting their work becomes critical to preserving their reputation and market position.

Ultimately, brand protection turns creative endeavors into sustainable revenue streams. By securing trademarks, copyrights, or patents, artists can explore opportunities in licensing, merchandising, or partnerships, confident that their rights are legally shielded.

These protections don't just guard against misuse; they also lay the groundwork for building long-term value. Let's look at how creative work can evolve into a business asset.

Art as an Asset

As artists navigate their careers, they often realize that their creations can transform from mere expressions into significant business assets (Aaker, 1996). This realization bolsters their artistic credibility instead of undermining it. Viewing art as a valuable asset, especially once it gains recognition, leads to profoundly rewarding experiences.

Artist Example: Let's look at J.K. Rowling and the Harry Potter franchise. What began as a single book concept blossomed into a global phenomenon encompassing films, merchandise, theme parks, and theatrical productions (Tetzeli, 2016). Rowling's proactive approach in protecting her intellectual property from the very beginning allowed her to guide the brand's expansion, ensuring every initiative aligned with her creative vision. Today, Harry Potter exists not just as a beloved story but as a multibillion-dollar entity.

Recognizing the economic potential in creative work often sparks the shift from passion to entrepreneurship. Photographers monetize through print sales, licensing, and brand partnerships, building both visibility and brand identity.

Diversifying income streams strengthens businesses. Graphic designers might craft logos or design patterns for fashion lines, broadening their reach and stability.

Strong partnerships amplify branding. When done right, companies recognize and reward the value artists bring. A well-crafted brand reflects both passion and professionalism.

Blending Both

Marrying creativity and commerce often demands a shift in perspective. Art should serve as both a display of talent and a testament to financial viability. Embracing the economic significance of artwork nurtures authenticity and inspires artists to create with fervor.

Navigating creativity and commerce can feel overwhelming due to pricing, contracts, and licensing. The key is self-education and expert advice. Platforms like Bandcamp help artists keep more earnings and build direct audience connections, showing the path to financial independence (Wikipedia, 2025).

Own Your Future

Artists who regard commerce as a partner rather than an obstacle open doors to broader outreach and deeper audience connections (Florida, 2019). By weaving business concepts into their practices, protecting their brand, and valuing art as an asset, they establish a robust foundation for enduring success (Kapferer, 2012).

As brand interactions with audiences flourish, these efforts yield tangible rewards. While artists don't need to adopt corporate structures, cultivating business acumen ensures that their expressions thrive amid a competitive landscape.

A strong brand is built on meaning, but it's protected through legal tools. That's where the IP ecosystem comes in.

1.3 IP Ecosystem

Trademarks, Copyrights, Patents

The IP ecosystem serves as the legal infrastructure for protecting creative and innovative output. Three primary tools, copyrights, trademarks, and patents, shape how creators can safeguard their work, brand identity, and inventions.

This section offers a high-level overview of each component, with dedicated chapters providing comprehensive guidance:

- **Copyrights** protect original works of authorship, such as music, writing, visual art, film, and digital content
- **Trademarks** secure brand identifiers like names, logos, and slogans, preserving brand recognition and preventing confusion in the marketplace
- **Patents** provide exclusive rights to inventors for their technical innovations, often encompassing the tools and technologies that underpin creative industries

Together, these pillars form the legal backbone of creative entrepreneurship. Each is explored in greater depth in the chapters that follow.

Creative Presence

In today's creative landscape, recognition isn't about shouting, it's about showing up consistently as yourself. Your work's look, sound, and feel leave an impression long before your name does. That's not branding for branding's sake; it's presence with intention.

Your creative identity is the thread running through everything you do: your perspective, process, and values. When clear and protected, it signals not just what you make, but what you stand for.

Let's explore how that thread evolves into lasting brand value.

Brand Growth

Marketing scholar Kevin Lane Keller developed a model called the Customer-Based Brand Equity Pyramid that maps out how a brand grows in the minds of its audience. While rooted in corporate marketing, the framework is incredibly useful for artists building their creative identity (Keller, 1993).

Here's how it translates:

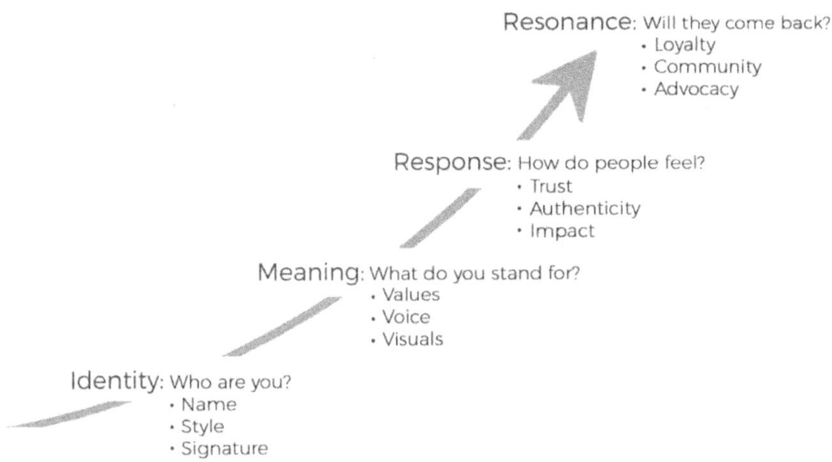

** Artist Tip: Brand equity is built on alignment; the consistency between who you are, what you express, and how people experience it.

One powerful real-world example of this model in action is Fenty, a brand that values its foundation.

● Fenty: Branding Inclusivity

When Rihanna launched Fenty Beauty, she didn't just release a makeup line; she redefined representation. With 40 foundation shades from the start, Fenty sent a powerful message of visibility and inclusion. What made it unforgettable wasn't just the range, but the alignment, every campaign, collaborator, and brand choice reinforced values of access, empowerment, and authenticity. The impact was intentional, consistent, and deeply human (Wischhover, 2017).

>> Artist Takeaway: Your work doesn't need to be loud to resonate. When your values shape what you create and how you share it, people don't just notice, they come back.

A strong brand is more than a logo; it is the emotional and strategic core of your identity. By building a brand with intention and protecting it through intellectual property tools like trademarks, artists can claim space in the marketplace and shape how their work is perceived. Branding is the foundation of visibility, recognition, and long-term creative power.

Now that we've explored how values-driven branding resonates with audiences, it's time to translate those insights into your strategy.

Let's begin with this Brand Building Worksheet:

Brand Building Worksheet

Branding Toolkit

Brand Identity Guide

The Creative Shield Layers

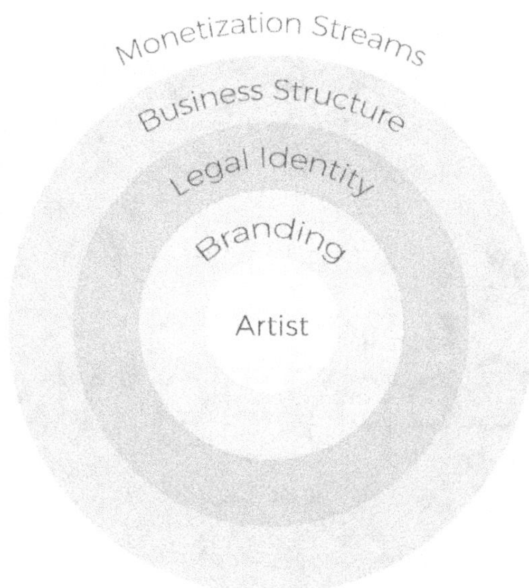

Core: Artist

Identity, Creative Purpose, Talent

Layer 2: Branding

Visuals, Name, Tone, Message

Layer 3: Legal Identity

Trademarks, Copyrights, Licensing

Layer 4: Business Structure

LLC, Contracts, Bank Account, EIN

Layer 5: Monetization Streams

Merchandise, Licensing, Digital, Services

Copyrights

Control Your Work

2.1 Copyright Basics

What is Copyright

Copyright is a powerful shield that empowers creators, giving them the authority to control the destiny of their original work. This legal right allows them to decide how their masterpieces are used, shared, and distributed, embracing forms of expression like literature, music, visual arts, films, and software. In essence, copyright is a guardian for one's intellectual property, ensuring that work cannot be replicated, sold, or altered without consent.

© = Copyright Symbol

Unlike trademarks, which protect names and logos, or patents that safeguard inventions, copyright hones in on the unique expression of an idea, not the idea itself. Copyright protection kicks in when a work is made tangible, whether scrawled on paper, stored digitally, or recorded.

While registering with the Copyright Office is not a prerequisite for copyright existence, doing so unlocks additional legal perks. For instance, to seek financial recompense for infringement, the copyright must be formally filed and registered (Cornell Copyright Information Center, 2023).

Not all creative works are protected by copyright; some are freely available for public use. These works fall into what's known as the public domain, offering artists a rich source of inspiration without legal restrictions.

** Artist Tip: Before remixing or referencing older works, double-check whether they're in the public domain; don't assume a vintage look means it is free to use.

Copyright vs. Public Domain

Many assume everything online is free to use, but most creative works are protected by copyright. Still, some works belong to the public domain and can be used without permission.

What is the Public Domain

The public domain is a rich source of works free from copyright, open for anyone to use, adapt, or transform. Works enter it through several paths:

1. The expiration of copyright – In the U.S., any work published before 1929 is now part of the public domain. For more recent creations, copyright endures for the creator's lifetime plus 70 years, or 95 years for corporate-owned works
2. Government works – Any publication from the federal government, including NASA images and Supreme Court rulings, automatically enters the public domain
3. Voluntary dedication – Creators can choose to abandon their copyright, willingly placing their work into the public domain

Public domain works are invaluable for remixes, educational endeavors, seminars, and so much more, allowing these creations to be used freely without fear of infringing upon someone else's intellectual property.

● The Public Domain and Sherlock Holmes

The iconic Sherlock Holmes stories by Sir Arthur Conan Doyle, written between 1887 and 1927, have largely entered the public domain, allowing creators to adapt and reimagine them freely. A 2020 ruling confirmed that even the final protected stories were now public domain, clearing the way for unrestricted use (*Meyer v. Conan Doyle Estate Ltd., 2020*).

>> Artist Takeaway: Public domain works like *Sherlock Holmes* are creative launchpads, free to adapt, remix, and make your own.

What Copyright Protects

Copyright embraces a diverse spectrum of expression, yet not every creation qualifies for this protection. Basic facts, ideas, and common phrases stand outside its reach. According to U.S. copyright law, the following categories of work receive safeguarding:

1. Literary Works

This realm includes books, poems, articles, blogs, and software code. As long as the work is original and captured in some format, it enjoys copyright protection. A blog post you craft today is automatically protected, regardless of registration status.

2. Musical Works

Music claims copyright protection in two distinct dimensions:

- The composition, which encompasses melody, lyrics, and sheet music
- The sound recording, which represents a particular rendition of a song

If a singer decides to cover a song, they must request permission from its copyright holder, yet their version is recognized as its separate copyright.

3. Dramatic Works and Screenplays

Copyright extends to screenplays, stage productions, and theatrical scripts. For example, a Broadway play cannot be transformed into a film without the playwright's consent.

4. Choreographic Works and Dance

Documentation in a written or recorded fashion is required for a dance routine to qualify for copyright. Improvised performances lack protection unless they are captured in some way. While Michael Jackson's iconic "moonwalk" isn't copyrightable, a fully choreographed segment of his performance is protected.

5. Visual Arts

Original artwork, including paintings, digital illustrations, sculptures, and photographs, is covered by copyright. This means that visual art created by both novices and experienced artists cannot be used or reproduced without the creator's explicit permission. The essence of copyright hinges on originality, not the artist's skill level.

6. Films and Audiovisual Works

Movies, documentaries, and videos crafted for social media find protection under copyright. The entirety of a film, including individual frames or stills, benefits from copyright safeguards.

7. Architectural Works

Buildings that feature unique designs that go beyond basic structures are covered under copyright. Any artistically styled house or building cannot be replicated without the creator's approval.

Knowing what copyright protects is one thing; formally registering your work gives you the legal power to enforce those rights.

2.2 Registering a Copyright

Why Registration Matters

Your work is protected at inception, but registration provides a public record and is required to enforce your rights in court. It's a straightforward process through the U.S. Copyright Office's eCO system. Follow these steps to get started:

Filing a Copyright

1. Identify Work
Select work type: Literary, Musical, Visual, Dramatic, or Audiovisual

2. Collect Information
Gather title, author, year, publication date, description, and ownership details.

3. Online Application
Go to copyright.gov -> Register a Copyright -> Choose category (single or batch)

4. Submit Work
Upload digitally. If physical, send a hard copy to the Library of Congress

5. Pay Fee
Fees vary by type and method: online payment is cheaper and faster

6. Receive Certificate
Approved submissions receive an official certificate

With your application prepared, the next step is to understand how long the process will take, what stages it involves, and the potential costs you may incur along the way.

Copyright Costs and Timelines

The cost of copyright registration is influenced by the type of work and how you choose to submit it. Here's a straightforward breakdown of typical fees (U.S. Copyright Office, 2023):

Registration Type	Fee	Notes
Single Application (one work by one author)	$45	Best for solo creators submitting one original work.
Standard Online Application (multiple authors or works)	$65	Most commonly used; suitable for more complex authorship.
Paper Application	$125	Slower and more expensive; used when online submission is not feasible.
Group Registration (e.g., photos, serials, newsletters)	$85–$500	Fee varies by group type and size; ideal for batch submissions.

Online processing is generally quick but varies in speed. Most online applications are processed within approximately 3 to 8 months, whereas paper submissions might take up to 16 months (U.S. Copyright Office, 2023). For urgent needs, expedited registrations are available for an additional fee, offering a lifeline for time-sensitive circumstances, such as impending legal issues.

Copyright Reversion

U.S. law allows authors to reclaim rights to works they previously transferred after 35 years, a process called copyright reversion, offering long-term leverage for songwriters, authors, and visual artists (17 U.S.C. § 203).

The "My Sweet Lord" Infringement Case

A landmark case highlighting the importance of copyright awareness is George Harrison's "My Sweet Lord" (1970), which bore a strong resemblance to The Chiffons' 1963 song "He's So Fine." In 1971, Bright Tunes Music Corp., the copyright holder, sued Harrison for infringement. The court ruled that although the copying wasn't intentional, Harrison had "subconsciously" borrowed the melody. He was ordered to pay $1.6 million in damages (*Bright Tunes Music Corp. v. Harrisongs Music, 1976).*

>> Artist Takeaway: Had The Chiffons' "He's So Fine" not been properly registered, establishing ownership in court would have been a daunting task. This case serves as a crucial reminder of the essential role formal copyright registration plays in safeguarding your creative endeavors.

This case underscores several important aspects:

- The registered work made enforcement more straightforward by establishing clear ownership
- The case showed that even accidental copying can still result in infringement
- Well-known artists must still navigate copyright risks
- Echoing a protected work, even unintentionally, can lead to legal action.

Understanding your rights is one thing; knowing how to enforce them, or when exceptions apply, is the next step.

2.3 Infringement & Fair Use

Protecting Artistic Identity

Before exploring infringement and enforcement, it's worth noting that U.S. visual artists have a unique protection beyond standard copyright: the Visual Artists Rights Act (VARA) (United States Congress, 1990). VARA grants moral rights, including the right to claim authorship, prevent distortion or misuse of the artist's name, and protect certain works from destruction even after sale, preserving the integrity of the work long-term.

● The Graffiti Warehouse Case

A defining case is *Cohen v. G&M Realty* (2018), in which a group of aerosol artists sued the developers of 5Pointz, a graffiti-covered warehouse in New York that was destroyed despite its recognized artistic value. The court found that the destruction of the murals violated VARA, awarding the artists $6.75 million in damages. The case set a powerful precedent that visual expression deserves both protection and respect, even when it's not hanging in a gallery.

What is Infringement

Copyright infringement occurs when someone uses, shares, or displays a creative work without permission, whether intentional or not. These exclusive rights require others to seek authorization unless an exception like fair use applies.

Examples include:

- Distributing a film, book, or song without consent
- Using copyrighted music in a YouTube video without a license
- Selling merch with unlicensed characters (e.g., Disney)
- Posting art or photos online without credit or permission

Even personal or nonprofit use can be infringement. A common misconception is that a lack of profit excuses unauthorized use, but U.S. law says otherwise (Stanford University Libraries, 2023).

Understanding Fair Use

While copyright law is strong, it makes space for artistic freedom through fair use. Fair use allows limited use of copyrighted work without permission when used for things like commentary, education, parody, or critique, balancing protection with expression (Stanford Copyright and Fair Use Center, 2023). (See Copyrights Toolkit for Fair Use Evaluation Worksheet.)

Four key factors determine fair use cases:

1. Purpose – Educational, non-commercial, or transformative use
2. Nature – Factual content is more eligible than works of art
3. Amount – Use less, especially if it's not the core of the original
4. Market Impact – If it hurts the original's market, fair use is unlikely

Fair Use Example: A film critic reviewing a movie can quote brief sections from the film without permission. In contrast, uploading an entire scene runs the risk of copyright infringement.

Copyright Infringement Example: Copying a design without changes or credit usually infringes, unless transformative. Platforms like YouTube use tools to flag potential violations.

(For enforcement tools like cease-and-desist letters, DMCA takedowns, and licensing steps, see Sections 6.1 and 6.2.)

These distinctions have played out in real-world courtrooms, where even short musical phrases have led to high-profile legal battles.

** Artist Tip: When in doubt, ask: *Am I adding new meaning, or just copying?* If it's not transformative, seek permission or use original content.

The "Dark Horse" Case

The 2020 Dark Horse case, where Katy Perry was sued by Christian rapper Flame, raised questions about how small musical elements can lead to copyright disputes. Flame alleged that Perry's hit copied an eight-note beat from his earlier song Joyful Noise. While a jury initially awarded $2.8 million in damages, the verdict was overturned, with the court ruling that the shared musical elements were too commonplace to qualify for protection (*Gray v. Perry, 2020*).

>> Artist Takeaway: The case sparked debate over how much borrowing is too much, especially with short beats or melodies, and reminded artists to tread carefully when inspired by existing work.

Ed Sheeran and Thinking Out Loud

In 2023, Ed Sheeran faced accusations that his hit "Thinking Out Loud" copied elements of Marvin Gaye's "Let's Get It On" *Griffin v. Sheeran*, No. 1:17-cv-05221 (S.D.N.Y. 2023). While Sheeran won, the case reignited debate over how much musical similarity is too much. The court ruled that the shared chord progression and rhythm weren't distinctive enough to constitute infringement (Sisario, 2023).

This contrasts with the *Blurred Lines* case (see 6.2), showing how music infringement claims remain unpredictable and shaped by jury perceptions of style and inspiration.

The "Hope" Poster Controversy

Shepard Fairey's iconic Hope poster for Barack Obama's 2008 campaign sparked legal controversy when he used a copyrighted photo by AP photographer Mannie Garcia without permission (*Associated Press v. Fairey,* 2011). Although Fairey initially denied it, he later admitted to using the image, resulting in an out-of-court settlement (Sherman, 2011).

The case raised key questions about fair use and transformative art, illustrating that even heavily altered images can still infringe if the original remains identifiable.

>> Artist Takeaway: Fair use is not guaranteed. When in doubt, get permission or a license. Copyright holders, including news outlets and photographers, actively enforce their rights.

MYTH BUSTER: "The Poor Man's Copyright"

MYTH: "If I mail myself my script, song, or sketch in a sealed envelope and don't open it, it's protected!"

TRUTH: Mailing your work to yourself does not create legal copyright protection. Courts do not recognize this as valid proof of ownership or authorship.

A postmarked envelope is easy to fake or alter, and it carries no legal weight in a copyright dispute. If your work is important enough to protect, it's worth registering it properly with the U.S. Copyright Office.

What Works:

Register your work with the U.S. Copyright Office. It's the only way to:

- Secure a public record of ownership
- Gain the right to sue for infringement
- Collect statutory (enacted by law) damages and attorney's fees

** Artist Tip: Your work deserves more than a $0.73 stamp and a myth that won't hold up in court.

Protect Your Work

Copyright protects more than just ideas; it protects the life you've built. From securing your rights at inception to defending your work through registration and fair use, understanding copyright is the first line of defense for any artist. Ownership is not just a concept; it's a legal reality that strengthens your ability to control, protect, and profit from your work.

Copyrights Toolkit

Copyright Application

Song Copyright Form

Fair Use Worksheet

AP Original vs. Obama Hope Poster
(*AP vs. Fairey, 2011*)

Trademarks

Protect Your Brand

3.1 What Can Be Trademarked

Trademark law, governed by the United States Patent and Trademark Office (USPTO), acts as a protective shield, helping you guard your unique identity, avoid brand confusion, and preserve your reputation, as well as the emotional connection your audience builds with your work.

Trademarks (or marks) are not just for corporations; they're vital for musicians, visual artists, designers, and performers. From your stage name and logo to signature packaging or color palette, trademarks are your first defense against creative theft (USPTO, 2023).

1. Word Marks

Word marks encompass the names, slogans, and phrases that embody your brand. These are often the first impressions people have, and the most susceptible to imitation.

▒ Artist Examples:

- Billie Eilish trademarked her name across music, fashion, and wellness, preserving its cultural and sonic legacy (USPTO, 2019)
- Virgil Abloh's OFF-WHITE includes trademarks for its name, quotation marks, and industrial font style as part of its visual identity (Abloh, 2017)
- Mitski secured trademarks for her name covering merch, tour branding, and album packaging to protect her presence across platforms (USPTO, 2025)

** Artist Tip: Artists should embrace the opportunity to trademark their performance names, studio names, slogans, and album or collection titles when they enter the realm of commerce.

2. Logos and Symbols

Logos are powerful visual representations of an artist's essence. These symbols can become so intertwined with an individual or movement that their meaning transcends the visual, carrying profound emotional and cultural significance.

▒ Artist Examples:

- Jean-Michel Basquiat's crown motif is retained under trademark protection by the Basquiat estate, symbolizing the essence of Black royalty and artistic empowerment (Basquiat Estate, 2022)
- Solange's Saint Heron logo embodies not merely a creative agency and label, but a whole philosophy of Black futurism and avant-garde art, safeguarded by trademark law (Saint Heron, 2021)
- Takashi Murakami's cheerful flower symbol is universally recognized across various domains, including art, streetwear, and luxury collaborations, reinforcing his global visual narrative (Murakami Studio, 2020)

** Artist Tip: If your visual representation, whether drawn, typed, or designed, frequently showcases your work or merchandise, it is prudent to secure a trademark.

3. Packaging & Style Marks

Trademark protection can extend to consistent visual styles or packaging choices that allow audiences to recognize your work at first glance.

▒ Artist Examples:

- Kehinde Wiley's baroque floral backgrounds are signature elements that also enrich apparel and public displays; they are supported by common law trademark and copyright protections (Wiley, n.d.)
- Telfar Clemens' Shopping Bag, with its distinctive shape and minimalistic packaging, has transformed into a cultural artifact known as "the Bushwick Birkin," under trade dress (Telfar Global, 2021)

- Bjork's album packaging, featuring unique cases, typography, and disc art, serves as a visual narrative, allowing fans to associate her identity with her creative work, protected as a whole (One Little Independent Records, n.d.)

** Artist Tip: Distinct color palettes, framing, illustrative characters, and unique packaging methods can be registered if they separate your brand from others.

Trade Dress

Trade dress signifies the recognizable visual presentation of a product or experience, indicating its source without depending on a logo or name. In the realm of the arts, trade dress can include:

- A visual artist's signature framing technique or varnishing method
- A fashion designer's textured garment tags or bag designs
- A musician's distinct album format or tour booth arrangement

■ Artist Examples:

- FKA twigs' performance visuals, costumes, and marketing materials reflect a carefully curated aesthetic that could fall under trade dress protection (Young Turks, 2020)
- The standard packaging of Yayoi Kusama's Louis Vuitton collaborations, with her signature polka dot-covered boxes, serves as extensions of her visual identity protected by trade dress (Kusama Enterprise, 2022)
- Tyler Mitchell's recurring use of soft pastel hues and Southern Black portraiture manifests as his editorial trademark in magazines and exhibitions (Mitchell Studio, 2021)

** Artist Tip: If you consistently present your work, products, or packaging with a distinctive look that sets your brand apart, you may qualify for trade dress protection under trademark law.

Other Types of Trademarks

Trademarks can encompass a range of branding elements beyond the conventional. Some less common types include sounds, scents, and specific movements linked to a brand.

1. Sound Marks

Sounds can garner trademark protection if they are distinctly associated with a product or brand. Examples include:

- The roar of the MGM lion — played before MGM films
- The Intel jingle — characterized by a unique five-note melody linked to Intel processors
- The NBC chimes — known for their three-note sound associated with the NBC network

For artists driven by audio, sound trademarks can secure rights to distinct audio segments or theme songs.

2. Scent Marks

Scent trademarks are among the rarer categories. To qualify, scents must differentiate a brand rather than merely fulfill a functional role. For instance, plumeria-scented yarn received trademark status due to its distinctive brand association (Cowan, Liebowitz & Latman, 2023).

3. Motion Marks

Motion trademarks are another uncommon sector. Certain movements tied closely to a brand can receive protection if they are distinctly affiliated with that brand. For instance, the distinctive scissor door mechanism of Lamborghini is trademarked as a part of their brand identity.

▒ Artist Examples:

- Doja Cat: Registered her stage name for performances, apparel, and digital music to protect her growing brand (USPTO, 2021)
- Hanna-Barbera: The oldest, still active motion mark trademark registration in the United States (Peterson, 2021)
- Brent Faiyaz: Registered his name and merch branding to launch Sonder and promote exclusive fashion drops independently (USPTO, 2021)

** Artist Tip: Distinct sounds, scents, or movements tied to your brand can qualify for trademark protection, expanding your rights beyond names and visuals.

Trademark Myths

Despite their significance, trademarks are frequently shrouded in misunderstandings.

Common misconceptions include:

Myth: Trademarks are only for big brands.
Truth: Indie artists can trademark names and logos, too.

Myth: Trademarks expire quickly.
Truth: They can last forever with proper use and renewal.

Myth: A trademark covers everything.
Truth: It only protects your mark in the category you register.

Myth: You can trademark any word or phrase.
Truth: Generic terms aren't allowed, but unique ones are.

Myth: A trademark guarantees total protection.
Truth: It gives rights, but disputes can still happen.

Now that you've seen the wide range of trademark possibilities, it's time to focus on how to build a strong one that holds up in court.

3.2 Building a Strong Trademark

Building a strong trademark means choosing something distinctive, legally protectable, and hard to imitate. This section breaks down what makes a mark effective, how to avoid common mistakes, and the steps to secure and enforce your rights.

Common Law vs. Registered

Before we move on to building a strong trademark, it's important to know the difference between a common law trademark and a registered trademark. See an In-depth Trademark Types Worksheet in the Trademarks Toolkit.

Both types offer protection, but they're not created equal. Common law rights arise the moment you start using a brand name or logo in the marketplace, but they're limited in scope. A federal registration, on the other hand, gives you nationwide protection and much stronger legal backing. As an analogy: Common Law is a padlock; Registration is a security system.

● From Common Law to Trademark Power

Lisa Congdon, a visual artist celebrated for her hand-lettered quotes and bold patterns, built her following through blogs, social media, and Etsy. Initially relying on common law rights, she faced growing imitation of her recognizable style. To protect her brand, she pursued federal trademark registration for her name and design elements. This move strengthened her legal position and led to major licensing deals with Chronicle Books and Target, allowing her to grow confidently into new markets while safeguarding her identity (Congdon, 2021).

>> Artist Takeaway: Not all trademark protection is created equal. Before choosing your path, take a quick look at how common law compares to full registration; it's the difference between sketching in pencil and carving in stone.

Aspect	Common Law	Registered (USPTO)
How You Get It	Just start using your brand in public	File an application ($350) with the USPTO and get approval
Where It Protects	Only in places where you're actively known	Nationwide (and can be extended internationally)
Power Level	Basic shield — limited legal backup	Legal armor — exclusive rights + stronger enforcement
Symbol	(no registration) ™	(after registration) ®
Best For	Local gigs, early-stage creatives	Merch, licensing, streaming, cross-platform expansion

Traits of Strong Marks

A strong trademark is distinctive, memorable, and protected.

1. Distinctiveness

The strongest trademarks are those that truly stand out. Whether naming a project, brand, or business, the more unique your trademark, the stronger the protection. Here's a quick guide to the five main types, ranked from strongest to weakest:

- Fanciful marks are invented words with no prior meaning, like VERZUZ, coined for a music battle series (United States Patent and Trademark Office, n.d.). These marks receive the strongest trademark protection
- Arbitrary marks use words in unexpected ways. OFWGKTA (Odd Future Wolf Gang Kill Them All) combined familiar terms into a distinctive music and merch brand (United States Patent and Trademark Office, n.d.)
- Suggestive marks hint at a brand's essence without saying it directly. Saint Heron suggests creativity and vision while keeping its purpose open to interpretation (Saint Heron, 2021)

- Descriptive marks directly state what the product is, making them harder to protect. Cold and Creamy is too literal, while Art Girl Army gained protection through strong recognition (Art Girl Army, 2017)
- Generic terms are the weakest trademarks; they describe a whole category and can't be protected. Names like Poetry Club are too general to distinguish a brand

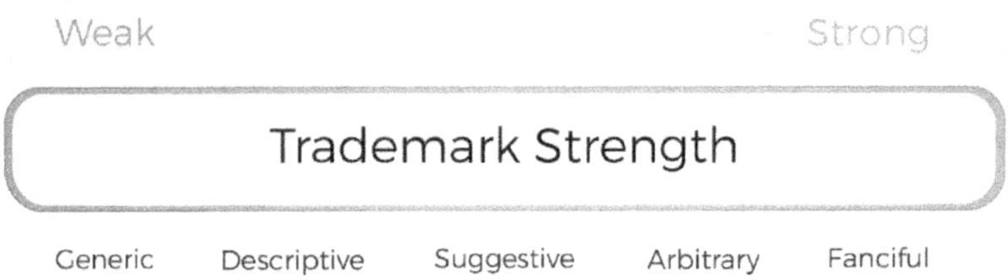

** Artist Tip: Secondary Meaning – Descriptive names like "Painter's Blend" aren't protected at first, but with consistent use and recognition, they can gain trademark protection as the name becomes tied to your brand.

2. Simplicity & Recall

A strong trademark is simple, memorable, and instantly recognizable. The Nike Swoosh is a perfect example: clean, clear, and iconic. Overly complex names or visuals can dilute your brand's impact.

3. Visual and Sound Appeal

The finest trademarks resonate through sound and design, combining visual appeal with functional clarity. A strong mark should maintain professionalism at any size, be easy to pronounce and spell, and avoid negative meanings across different languages.

Trademark Lifecycle

A trademark isn't protected by the idea alone; it takes clear steps from concept to registration to make it enforceable. Here's a quick overview:

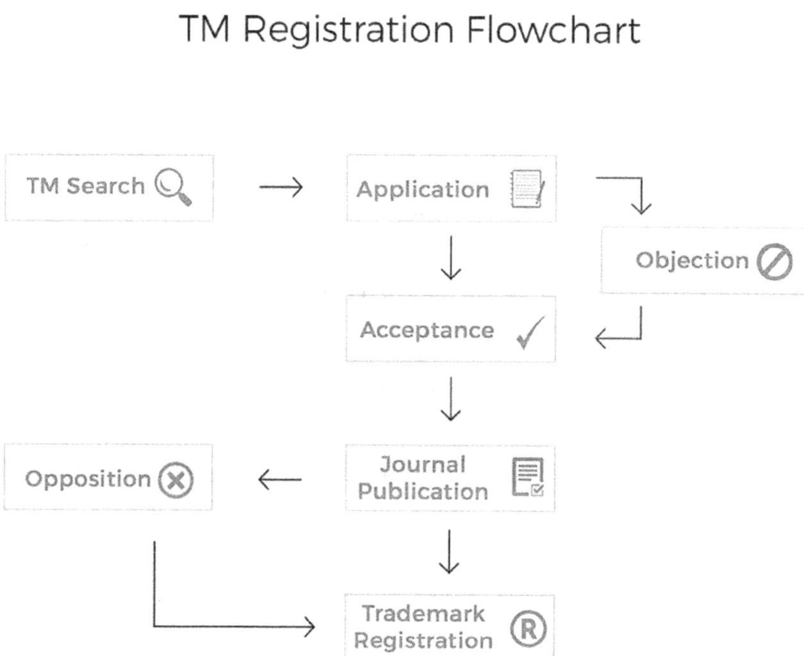

After mapping the process, here's a closer look at each stage:

- Create & Investigate - Choose a unique name, logo, or phrase and run a trademark search; this is the foundation of protection
- Submit Your Application - File with the USPTO, include a clear image or description of your mark, list the goods/services, and pay the fee

- Review & Publication - A USPTO examiner reviews your application; if unopposed, it advances
- Register & Protect - Once registered, your trademark is legally yours. Monitor it, enforce your rights, and renew every 10 years

What happens when a trademark isn't secured in time? The following case illustrates the risks of skipping legal safeguards, even for world-famous artists.

Banksy Trademark Battle

A major trademark dispute in the art world involved street artist Banksy, who faced legal challenges while trying to protect his work. Known for his provocative graffiti, Banksy encountered a hurdle when a greeting card company attempted to trademark one of his images, arguing that because he hadn't registered it, they had the right to use it (*Full Colour Black Ltd. v. Pest Control Office Ltd., 2022*).

Banksy's anonymity made it difficult to assert legal ownership, and his public stance, once claiming "copyright is for losers," further weakened his case. The court ruled that trademark protection requires a clear intent to commercialize, which Banksy hadn't demonstrated. As a result, he lost the case, highlighting the difficulties artists face in protecting their work when they avoid formal legal channels (WIPO, 2021).

>> Artist Takeaway: Artists should register trademarks early to prevent others from claiming their work. Trademarks also require proof of commercial use connected to a business or brand. Additionally, public statements against copyright can undermine an artist's legal position in trademark disputes.

As Banksy's experience shows, even iconic work can fall short of legal protection if the foundation isn't strong. Let's look at how to avoid the most common trademark pitfalls.

3.3 Avoiding Trademark Traps

As previously discussed, some trademarks are too weak to protect. Generic or descriptive names often fail in court or get rejected. This section explains why and how recognition can strengthen them, while highlighting what makes a trademark effective.

Generic & Descriptive Risks

Generic and descriptive marks are the weakest types of trademarks because they fail to distinguish your brand from others in the marketplace. Here's why they offer the least protection compared to stronger marks.

1. Generic: The Weakest Trademarks

A generic trademark refers to terminology commonly used to designate a type of product or service rather than a specific brand. These terms cannot be registered because they don't signify a unique source. For instance:

- "Bicycle" cannot be claimed as a trademark for bicycles
- "Pizza Shop" cannot be registered for a restaurant that serves pizza

Blocking generic terms from registration prevents any one company from monopolizing the common language. If "Coffee" were trademarked, other shops couldn't describe their product without risk. Some brands lost their trademarks after becoming generic terms:

- Escalator – Initially a trademark held by the Otis Elevator Company
- Aspirin – Formerly a protected trademark owned by Bayer
- Yo-Yo – Originally trademarked but later deemed generic

To avoid this, artists and businesses should choose unique, distinctive names that don't describe a product category.

2. Descriptive: A Risky Trademark Choice

Descriptive marks directly reference a product's qualities or features, making them hard to register since they don't clearly distinguish one brand from another. For example:

- "Soft and Warm" for blankets merely describes the product's attributes
- "Fast Printing" for a print shop conveys a characteristic of the service

However, if descriptive marks obtain recognized association, they may be eligible for trademark protection, unlike generic ones.

Recognized Association

A descriptive mark can gain trademark protection through "secondary meaning," when consumers associate it with a specific source through consistent use and recognition over time (USPTO, 2023).

Gaining Recognized Association

To establish a recognized association for a descriptive mark, the owner must show that consumers link the mark specifically to their brand. This can be demonstrated through:

- Long-term use – The brand has continuously employed the mark over an extended duration
- Extensive marketing – The mark has received significant exposure from marketing efforts
- Sales and feedback – Evidence that customers connect the mark specifically to the company, not just the product type

Trademarks with Recognized Association

Notable brands that started as descriptive but earned trademark protection through recognized association include:

- Holiday Inn – Originally a common phrase for places to stay, it evolved into a well-known brand
- ChapStick – Initially a generic term for lip balm, it came to signify a specific product
- American Airlines – Descriptive yet trademarked due to strong brand awareness

See the following case study below for a recognized association example illustrating how trademark protection can extend across industries:

The Legal Battle Over the "LV" Logo

Louis Vuitton sued a South Korean fried chicken restaurant, "Louis Vuiton Dak," for trademark infringement, arguing the name and branding closely mimicked its own. Although the restaurant claimed parody, the court found the similarities could mislead consumers and harm Louis Vuitton's reputation.

It reaffirmed that trademark protection can extend beyond industry boundaries when brand dilution is at risk. Louis Vuitton won the case, received damages, and the restaurant was ordered to rebrand (*Louis Vuitton Malletier S.A. v. Louis Vuiton Dak, 2023*).

>> Artist Takeaway: Trademarks are not just for luxury brands; they protect your identity. If someone uses a name or look that causes confusion or rides on your reputation, even under the guise of parody, your brand may be at risk without trademark protection.

Recognized association strengthens your mark; however, even strong brands can stumble without proper planning.

To stay protected and competitive, avoid the common mistakes that weaken trademark rights or invite legal trouble.

Avoiding Trademark Pitfalls

Trademark missteps can drain time, money, and momentum. This table outlines common mistakes, their impact, and how to avoid them.

Mistake	Why It's a Problem	Better Approach
Descriptive or Obvious Names	Generic names (e.g., *Delicious Cakes*) are weak and hard to protect legally.	Use suggestive, symbolic, or inventive names.
Skipping the TM Search	You risk legal conflicts or being forced to rebrand.	Use the USPTO search tool or hire an attorney.
Delaying Registration	Without registration, you don't legally "own" the mark. Others can claim it first.	File as soon as the brand is public.
Complex Names or Logos	Complicated marks are hard to remember and harder to defend legally.	Choose simple, catchy, and unique names or visuals.
Not Using the Mark	Rights can lapse or be challenged if a mark isn't used in commerce.	Start using the mark promptly in actual sales or branding.
Inconsistent Branding	Using different versions of a name/logo across platforms weakens legal protection.	Keep branding consistent across all materials and platforms.

While some trademarks fail, many succeed, especially when artists choose distinct, well-crafted marks. Here are a few creative wins worth studying.

Notable Trademark Wins

Powerful trademarks in the creative field often emerge from businesses and artists who choose distinctive, memorable, and legally sound marks, ones that not only stand out but also withstand legal scrutiny and imitation.

1. ● Disney: A Trademark Powerhouse

Disney has built one of the most robust trademark portfolios, encompassing its logo, character names, film titles, and even specific color schemes. The silhouette of Mickey Mouse, the Disney castle emblem, and characters like Elsa and Simba are all legally safeguarded.

2. ● Tiffany & Co.: Owning a Color

The signature Tiffany Blue used in the company's jewelry boxes is a registered trademark, preventing other jewelry brands from using that exact shade for packaging. While rare, color trademarks are possible when a color becomes uniquely tied to a brand's identity, as Tiffany's blue has with luxury and exclusivity (Tiffany & Co., n.d.).

>> Artist Takeaway: Artists and businesses can cultivate robust trademarks through thoughtful choices of distinct names, designs, and visual elements.

● Beyoncé's "Blue Ivy" Dispute

In 2012, Beyoncé and Jay-Z attempted to trademark "Blue Ivy Carter," but faced legal opposition from a Boston wedding planner who had already registered the name "Blue Ivy." While Beyoncé secured rights to the full name, she could not claim the standalone version (Ritson, 2019).

>> Artist Takeaway: Your name is personal, but in trademark law, it's also business. Priority matters more than fame. Register early, and protect your brand, even if it starts with your name.

• The Fight Over "The Slants" Trademark

A landmark trademark confrontation involved The Slants, an Asian-American band that sought trademark registration. Their 2011 application was denied by the USPTO under a law barring trademarks deemed offensive. The band argued they were reclaiming the term and that the denial violated their First Amendment rights (*Matal v. Tam, 2017*).

The case reached the U.S. Supreme Court, which ruled in favor of The Slants, holding that trademarks cannot be refused based on subjective notions of offensiveness, significantly impacting trademark law.

>> Artist Takeaway: Trademarks can't be denied for being provocative. The Slants' Supreme Court win affirmed that bold, culturally charged brand identities are protected under free expression and eligible for trademark rights.

Protect What You Create

These wins show what's possible when artistic identity is treated as a serious business asset. The bottom line is simple: creative identity isn't just something you build; it's something you protect. In a world where every brand competes for attention, your trademark is your stake in the ground, your voice in a crowded room, and your shield against being erased. However, waiting too long to claim that voice leaves the door open to "trademark squatters," those who register names they know artists are about to use, hoping to cash in on someone else's vision. Don't let hesitation become vulnerability. Protect your brand early and often.

Trademarks Toolkit

Trademark Strength List

USPTO Application Guide

Trademark Protection Sheet

Banksy's Original vs. Full Colour Black's Version

(*Full Colour Black Ltd. vs Pest Control Office Ltd., 2022*)

Used under fair use for educational and commentary purposes.

Trademark Readiness Checklist

Create a unique name, slogan, or logo

☐ Stands out from others
☐ Not a generic term (e.g., "Good Music", "Art Shop")

Check availability

☐ Searched USPTO or national registry
☐ Googled for existing use
☐ Checked social handles and domains

Define trademark class

☐ Identified correct category (apparel, education, music)

Prepare your application

☐ Logo or wordmark file ready
☐ Clear description of brand
☐ Correct class and jurisdiction selected

Plan for enforcement

☐ Set up a Google Alert for your name/logo
☐ Know how to send a cease-and-desist
☐ Monitor marketplaces and social media

Patents

Protect Innovation

4.1 Understanding Patents

This chapter is for artists who innovate with tools, techniques, and technology. While copyrights protect creative expression, patents cover inventions like sculpting tools, interactive displays, or digital art processes. Like copyrights, patents protect creative innovations, while trademarks protect brand identity.

What is a Patent

A patent grants you exclusive rights to your invention for about 20 years in exchange for publicly sharing how it works. It protects the tools and processes behind creativity, not the artwork itself (USPTO, 2023).

** Artist Tip: Copyright protects your creative works; patents protect inventions and processes. Use copyright for art and music, and consider a patent for tools, tech, or techniques. Knowing the difference ensures full protection.

Patent Criteria

To obtain patent protection, an invention must fulfill several key criteria:

- Novelty – The invention should be fresh and undisclosed
- Non-Obviousness – It should not be a simple extension of existing technologies
- Utility – The invention must have practical usefulness
- Patentable Subject Matter – Must be a recognized category like a process, machine, or composition

Artists can secure patent protection for new artistic tools, printing techniques, or distinctive sculpting materials.

Patent Types for Artists

Although patents are often associated with technology, they are increasingly vital for artists and designers crafting innovative artistic tools and methods.

The three main types of patents include:

1. Utility Patents

Utility patents cover inventive creations that are both novel and practically useful, or enhancements to existing processes involving machines or materials.

Examples of utility patents:

- Advanced digital art tools or software – A pioneering AI painting application
- Unique sculpting or printing techniques – An avant-garde 3D printing method
- Specialized art materials – An innovative, eco-friendly paint

For instance, a digital artist developing a unique AI algorithm for portrait enhancement could pursue a utility patent to protect the innovation.

2. Design Patents

Design patents focus on the ornamental aspects of a product rather than its functionality. This allows artists and designers to protect fresh aesthetic designs.

Examples of design patents:

- Original chair designs from industrial artists
- Unique jewelry designs featuring captivating shapes
- Sculptures emphasizing distinctive visual forms

Design patents remain valid for 15 years from issuance (USPTO, 2023), providing essential protection for fashion designers, furniture makers, and visual artists wanting to shield the appearance of their works.

3. Plant Patents

Though less applicable to many artists, plant patents safeguard new plant varieties that are artificially propagated. Floral designers and botanical artists may seek patents for novel hybrid flowers that showcase extraordinary colors and forms.

Understanding which type of patent fits your work is just the beginning; now, let's walk through the filing process.

4.2 Patent Application Process

Copyright protects creative works the moment they're born, while patents need a formal journey to blossom. The patent system empowers creators, allowing them to guard their inventions from being copied or exploited by others without their consent.

This section offers a clear pathway to navigate patent filing, highlighting timelines and financial aspects.

Filing a Patent

Acquiring a patent is an art in itself, demanding careful preparation and strict compliance with legal expectations. Here's a simplified roadmap for filing a patent with the United States Patent and Trademark Office.

Step 1: Verify Patentability

Before you dive in, ensure your invention shines with these three attributes: Novelty, Non-obviousness, and Utility.

For instance, inventing a new digital brush for graphic design could earn you a utility patent, provided it isn't too similar to what already exists.

Step 2: Patent Search

A patent search helps confirm your idea's originality. Use the USPTO database to spot similar inventions; too much overlap could mean rejection.

Many turn to patent attorneys or firms for thorough searches and expert guidance, helping spot overlaps, navigate databases, and boost approval odds with confidence.

Step 3: Choose Patent Type

Choose the patent that best captures the essence of your innovation as described earlier.

Step 4: Submit Application

You have two avenues:

- Provisional Patent (PPA): A 12-month placeholder that secures a filing date and lets you use "Patent Pending"
- Non-Provisional Patent (NPA): A full application reviewed by the USPTO, required for full patent protection

Most inventors start with a provisional application, giving them time to refine their concepts before making a formal entry.

Step 5: Prepare & File

Your patent application should encompass:

- A detailed narrative of your invention
- Claims that underscore its distinctiveness
- Relevant sketches or diagrams
- An affirmation from the inventor attesting to originality

Step 6: Review & Approval

After submission, a USPTO examiner reviews your application and may ask for edits. If rejected, you can revise or appeal.

Upon approval, the USPTO issues a patent grant, safeguarding your creation for up to 20 years (utility patent) or 15 years (design patent).

Patent Timelines

Stage	Typical Time
Filing to First Review	12–18 months
Review to Decision	18–36 months
Total Time to Patent	3–5 years

The patent approval journey can last anywhere from 12 months to several years, depending on the intricacy of the invention and the workload at the USPTO (USPTO, 2023).

Factors influencing the time it takes to secure patent approval include:

- Invention complexity: Patents that explore detailed technical aspects need more time for thorough evaluation
- Backlogs of examiners: The USPTO handles a vast number of patent submissions annually
- Amendments and appeals: A patent rejection can significantly delay the approval timeline

To speed things up, inventors can opt for the USPTO's *Track One Prioritized Examination*, a paid fast-track service that delivers a patent decision within 12 months, ideal for quick market entry, investor interest, or early licensing.

Patent Costs

The expenses associated with filing a patent fluctuate depending on application fees, attorney charges, and upkeep costs. Below is a detailed overview of the various financial obligations linked to patent applications (USPTO, 2023).

Expense	Estimated Cost
Provisional Patent Filing Fee	$75–$300
Utility Patent Filing Fee	$430–$1,500
Design Patent Filing Fee	$255–$1,020

- File a provisional patent application to secure an early filing date while postponing major expenses
- Qualify for USPTO fee reductions as a small or micro-entity to lower filing and maintenance costs
- Seek grants, sponsorships, or crowdfunding to help cover patent-related expenses

Taking early, strategic steps can help protect your innovation without straining your finances.

You've filed the paperwork, navigated the legal maze, and secured your patent. Now what? For artists, a patent isn't just a legal shield; it's a launchpad. It opens the door to income, partnerships, and new opportunities, all while keeping ownership in your hands.

The next section shows how to turn your protected idea into a profit-generating asset through smart licensing, strategic partnerships, and creative control.

4.3 Licensing & Monetizing Patents

Licensing innovative tools or processes helps artists increase income and brand reach while retaining ownership, yet it invites legal risks, like patent trolls. This section covers how to license effectively, avoid common pitfalls, and learn from people who have turned their ideas into income.

How to License Your Patent

Patent licensing allows others to use or sell your invention in exchange for royalties or fees. It offers a way to earn income without managing production or distribution, freeing you to focus on new ideas.

There are two main types of licensing agreements: exclusive and non-exclusive. An exclusive license gives one party full rights to your invention, while a non-exclusive license allows multiple users access, each paying for the privilege. Knowing which model fits your goals is crucial.

For example, A graphic designer develops a unique digital brush and licenses it to several software companies. As a non-exclusive deal, the designer earns royalties from each user while retaining ownership of the invention. (See 5.2 Licensing for Profit).

Of course, licensing isn't just about making a deal; it's about making the right deal. Successful agreements require strategy and follow-through.

** Artist Tip: Before signing a patent license, define how your invention can be used, for how long, and in what markets. Clear terms protect your creativity and maximize your earning potential.

The patent license process includes key steps to protect rights and turn innovation into opportunity. The following chart outlines some key steps to successfully getting your patent licensed.

Patent License Process

1. Confirm Ownership
Know your rights before licensing

2. Identify Licencees
Find ideal users for your invention

3. Define Strategy
Choose your licensing model

4. Setting Key Terms
Establish fees, rights and duration

5. Prepare Materials
Create clear, compelling documentation

6. Draft Agreement
Protect terms with legal support

7. Negotiate Terms
Address questions and finalize the deal

8. Monitor Compliance
Ensure licensee follows your terms

Artist Takeaway: Licensing your patent turns ownership into opportunity, each step protects your rights while opening doors to revenue and reach.

Pantone Case Study

The Pantone Color Matching System revolutionized art, design, and manufacturing by standardizing how colors are identified and reproduced. Before Pantone's innovation, artists and designers struggled with color inconsistencies that complicated their work and production processes (Budds, 2015). Pantone's breakthrough brought precision to creativity, bridging the gap between vision and execution.

Pantone's patented color matching process empowered artists, printers, and manufacturers to replicate colors with precision. It set a new standard across design, fashion, branding, and production, transforming color from subjective art to reproducible science and expanding creative possibilities worldwide.

>> Artist Takeaway: Although Pantone's original patents have since expired, the company strategically protects its proprietary color formulas through trade secrets and trademark registrations (refer to 5.1 Contracts in IP Protection). Pantone's approach highlights several key lessons for artists and innovators:

- Use patents strategically to secure a market advantage, even if only for a limited time
- Layer multiple forms of IP protection, patents, trade secrets, and trademarks, to sustain influence after patents expire
- Adopt or create patented systems to build authority and legacy within your field

Pantone's success story illustrates how thoughtful patenting, combined with ongoing protection strategies, can transform industries and position artists for long-term impact.

As valuable as patents can be, they can also attract the wrong kind of attention, especially from entities looking to exploit the system.

Patent Trolls & Risks

While patents can be lucrative, they also attract patent trolls who exploit the system, so artists must remain alert to legal threats.

1. What Are Patent Trolls

- Patent trolls (non-practicing entities) use patents to sue rather than innovate
- Often hold vague or broad patents to claim wide rights
- Target small creators with limited legal defense
- File lawsuits seeking large settlements without making products

2. Protect Against Trolls

To avoid legal disputes and baseless infringement claims, patent holders should:

- Define Your Patent Clearly – Precise claims help prevent frivolous lawsuits; a patent attorney ensures a patent is legally solid
- Monitor Industry Trends – Spot infringement early; start with a cease-and-desist before legal action, (*see* 6.2)
- Join Anti-Troll Groups – Organizations like EFF and Unified Patents fight unjust lawsuits and support inventors

Artists with Patents

Some artists extend their creativity into invention, securing patents to protect tools, systems, and innovations they've developed along the way. Here are a few notable examples, showing how creative problem-solving can lead to lasting recognition and revenue.

Artist Examples:

- Eddie Van Halen invented a device that allowed guitarists to play hands-free with enhanced control. U.S. Patent No. 4,656,917 (1987)
- Hedy Lamarr co-developed a signal-hopping invention that laid the groundwork for Wi-Fi and Bluetooth. U.S. Patent No. 2,292,387 (1942)
- Marlon Brando created a mechanism for evenly tightening drumheads to improve sound quality. U.S. Patent No. 6,812,392 (2004)
- Harry Connick Jr. designed a digital system for displaying and annotating sheet music during live performances. U.S. Patent No. 6,348,648 (2002)
- Michael Jackson invented a shoe system that allowed performers to lean forward beyond their center of gravity for stage performances. U.S. Patent No. 5,255,452 (1993)

These artist-inventors prove that protecting tools and technologies can open new avenues for control, licensing, and revenue (Nolan Heimann LLP, 2021). (See these patent sketches in the Patents Toolkit.)

LEGO Design Patent

LEGO, the famed toy manufacturer, is a prime example of how strategic design protection can defend a brand's identity. LEGO religiously protects its iconic minifigure design, using design patents to ward off competitors and imitators.

The company actively enforces its rights, taking legal action against brands that attempt to replicate its beloved mini-characters, including a notable case against ZURU Inc. in 2020 (*LEGO A/S v. ZURU Inc., 2020*).

>> Artist Takeaway: Major companies invest heavily in original designs and defend them fiercely. Artists can protect their innovations the same way, building stronger brands and opportunities.

Vantablack Case

British-Indian artist Anish Kapoor obtained exclusive rights to Vantablack, recognized as the blackest pigment, absorbing 99.96% of light (Delaney, 2016).

Controversy and Public Response

- Kapoor's exclusive rights barred other artists from using Vantablack, igniting a global discourse on artistic control over color
- In reaction, artist Stuart Semple created alternative ultra-black pigments, making them available to the public, contesting Kapoor's claim

Insights from the Vantablack Case

- Exclusive licensing can spark debate when it limits artistic expression
- Artists should consider the broader implications of exclusive agreements
- Patent ownership holds power but demands ethical considerations

>> Artist Takeaway: The Vantablack case exemplifies how patents can shape artistic innovation while posing ethical questions about ownership.

The Vantablack debate reminds us that invention isn't just about what's new, it's about how you protect it. Here's the bottom line for artists embracing innovation.

Innovation is Power

Patents don't just protect inventions; they protect vision. For artists and innovators, understanding patent law means taking control of how ideas move through the world. Protect what you create, and build not just art, but legacy.

Patents Toolkit

Marlon Brando

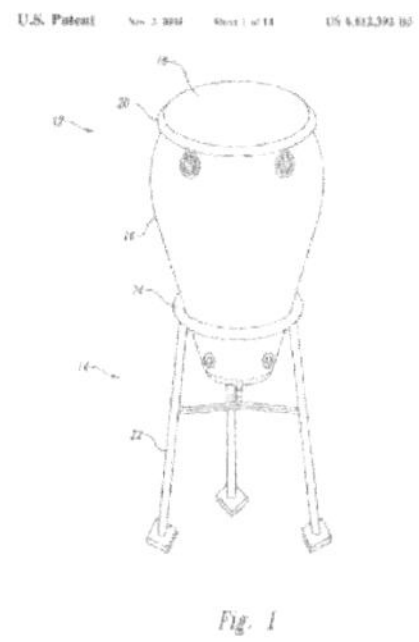

Eddie Van Halen

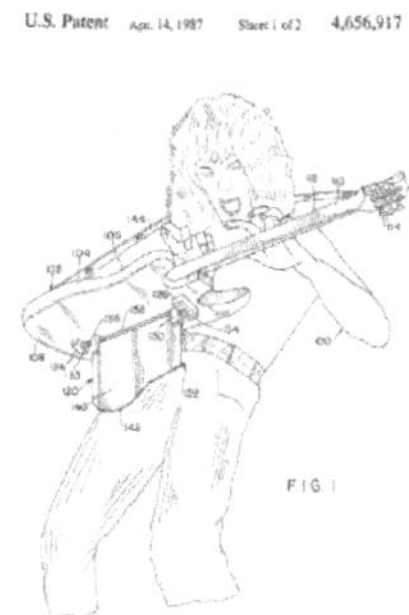

Michael Jackson

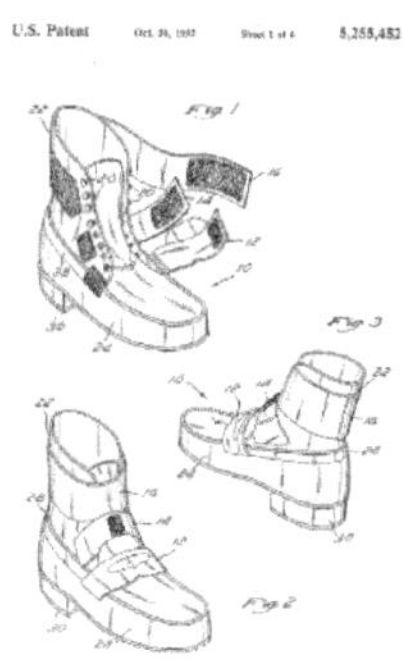

Hedy Lamarr

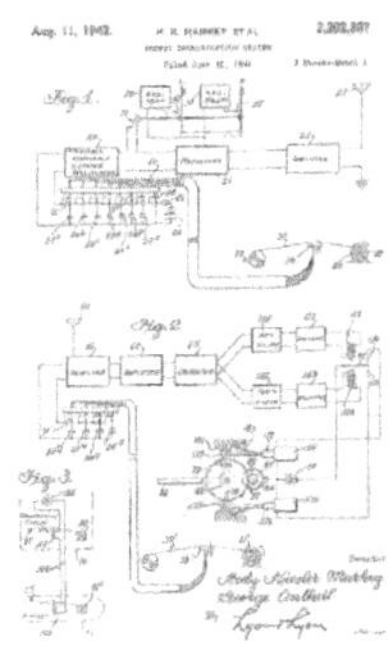

Harry Connick Jr.

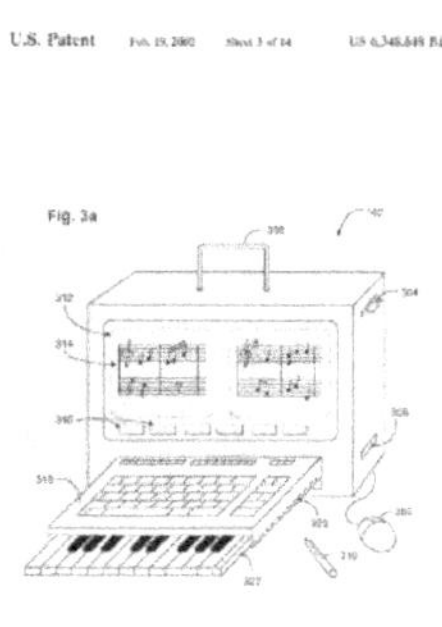

USPTO registrations of featured patents

Contracts

Protect Your Work

5.1 Contracts in IP Protection

Contracts are essential for protecting intellectual property and ensuring fair compensation. From licensing and collaborations to commissioned work, clear written agreements help artists avoid misunderstandings and legal issues. This section covers key contract types, essential terms, and red flags to watch for.

Why Written Agreements Matter

Many artists work on trust, relying on verbal agreements or handshake deals. However, without a written contract, you have little legal protection if disputes arise over payment, ownership, or usage rights. A contract defines who owns what, when payment is due, and how the work can be used.

Recent laws like New York City's Freelance Isn't Free Act reflect a growing recognition of these risks, requiring written contracts and timely payment for freelance work (New York City Department of Consumer and Worker Protection [DCWP], 2023). Even if your state doesn't offer these protections, your contract can. Always define scope, include payment terms, and outline what happens if things go wrong.

Written agreements ensure you maintain control of your work and are paid for it. The following are two of the most common contract types, and how to protect your rights in each.

Licensing & Work-for-Hire

Contracts should be comprehensive and straightforward, highlighting essential components to prevent misinterpretation. Here are crucial clauses to incorporate in every licensing or work-for-hire agreement:

1. Ownership Terms

Ownership is key in any contract. Without a written agreement, artists keep copyright by default, unless the agreement is a work-for-hire, where the client owns the rights.

- Licensing Agreement – You retain ownership while granting specific usage rights to the licensee
- Work-for-Hire Agreement – The client obtains complete rights to the work upon completion

Always clarify if you are licensing or fully transferring rights. If you are giving up ownership, negotiate higher pay to match the forfeited value.

2. Compensation Terms

Contracts must set clear payment terms, encompassing:

- Upfront fees or milestone-based payments
- Royalties from licensing (e.g., a percentage of sales)
- Kill fees (compensation if the client cancels the project)
- Late payment penalties (to ensure prompt payment)

If you license artwork to a clothing brand, the agreement should delineate how royalties are calculated, specifying whether you earn a percentage from each sale or a flat fee, along with the payment schedule.

3. Scope & Restrictions

Defining how your artwork can be used safeguards against unintended exploitation. This part should clarify:

- The venues and methods of display or sale (e.g., online, print, merchandise)
- Whether the client possesses exclusive or non-exclusive rights
- If the licensee can alter the work
- Geographic limitations (e.g., regional or global use)

For instance, if you license a book cover design, you might restrict its use to print distribution, prohibiting merchandise applications (like shirts or posters) unless additional compensation is agreed upon.

4. Confidentiality & Trade Secrets

As an artist, your process is often just as valuable as the final product. From your unique editing style to pricing strategies, pitch decks, or unreleased collections, these elements can be considered trade secrets if they give you a competitive edge and are kept confidential.

Your contracts should include confidentiality clauses that prevent others from disclosing, sharing, or using this sensitive information without your permission. This is especially crucial when:

- Sharing rough drafts or concept artwork with a potential collaborator or client
- Pitching a new idea, script, or design collection to a company
- Revealing client lists or business strategies during a partnership discussion
- Giving access to internal documents, tools, or systems as part of a project or licensing deal

You can use a separate non-disclosure agreement (NDA) before discussions or sharing materials to protect your ideas. It is a safeguard for non-public creative work. (See the Contracts Toolkit for the Trade Secrets & NDA Cheat Sheet.)

Example: Let's say you choreograph a dance sequence with an original fusion technique. If you share that method with a brand before signing a contract, and they replicate it without credit or payment, you may have no recourse unless you had a confidentiality agreement in place.

** Artist Tip: If something is private, valuable, and gives you an edge, protect it. Your behind-the-scenes brilliance deserves just as much legal coverage as the final masterpiece.

5. Duration & Termination

Contracts should outline:

- The duration of the licensing agreement
- The conditions and process for early termination
- The agreement is renewable after expiration
- Any notice requirements for renewal or termination

▩ Artist Example: In 2022, Kellie Day licensed her artwork under a contract that allowed either party to end the agreement if no sales occurred within 12 months. This clause protected her ability to regain full rights and explore other opportunities if the partnership didn't perform (Day, 2022).

6. Dispute & Liability Clauses

In the event of disagreements, contracts should incorporate:

- Arbitration or mediation clauses to handle disputes outside of court
- Indemnification clauses to protect against legal claims related to your work
- A jurisdiction clause to establish which laws govern the contract
- Each party's responsibilities in the event of a legal dispute

For instance, if you create a public installation, the contract should limit your liability if someone is injured while engaging with the artwork, especially when the venue controls the space, manages crowd flow, or is responsible for safety measures like lighting, signage, or physical barriers. Without this clause, you could be exposed to claims arising from hazards you didn't create or control.

Contracts aren't just formalities; they protect your rights, income, and creative control when structured clearly and thoughtfully.

Contract Hazards

Spotting pitfalls helps you avoid unfair terms that may limit your rights, control, or income. Recognizing risks early can prevent costly mistakes. The diagram below highlights key risk levels (see more Contract Red Flags in the Contracts Toolkit).

Agreement Risk Levels

Deal-Killers
- Work-for-hire traps
- Moral rights waivers
- Perpetual rights

Non-Negotiable
- IP ownership
- Attribution
- Indemnification

Negotiable
- Payment
- Timeline
- Exclusivity

Artist Tip: Know what to protect, adjust, or refuse before you sign.

Client List as Trade Secret

In 2018, acclaimed gallery Lehmann Maupin filed a lawsuit against a former employee who joined a competing gallery, alleging she took confidential client lists, sales histories, and private deal terms. While no artwork was stolen, the court recognized this insider information as a valuable trade secret, protected under the NDA she had signed during her employment (*Lehmann Maupin v. Yoo, 2018*).

>> Artist Takeaway: Your client list, pricing, and pitches can be more valuable than the art itself. When sharing them, use an NDA or confidentiality clause, protecting your creative ecosystem is part of true professionalism.

Trade secrets aren't the only risk. Licensing agreements themselves, especially when enforced too aggressively, can backfire, as the next case shows.

Tintin Licensing Dispute

What happens when protecting art begins to suppress creative freedom? Fans and scholars of Hergé's Tintin faced this dilemma when Moulinsart S.A., the foundation managing his legacy, enforced strict licensing rules, even targeting educational use. In 2015, a Belgian court ruled that the foundation wrongly demanded fees, affirming that some Tintin works qualified for copyright exceptions in academic contexts.

The case highlighted the risks of overly restrictive licensing and the importance of fair use rights ("Tintin fan club wins legal fight with Hergé heirs over image rights," 2015).

>> Artist Takeaway

- Artists should push for fair licensing to protect their rights
- Rights holders must enforce licenses without limiting creative freedom
- Independent artists should stay alert to overreach by larger IP owners

The Right of Publicity

Your identity is just as valuable as your artwork, and contracts are one of the most powerful tools for protecting both. The Right of Publicity grants you legal control over how your name, image, voice, likeness, and persona are used in commercial settings.

Whether you're a visual artist featured in a gallery catalog, a musician in a video, or a model in a fashion campaign, this right shields you from unauthorized use in ads, merchandise, media, or promotional content. It ensures that your identity isn't exploited without your permission or proper compensation.

Unlike copyrights or trademarks, you don't need to register your right of publicity. But you do need to actively enforce it, particularly through well-drafted contracts. Any time you are part of a shoot, recording, or project, your agreement should clearly state:

- Where and how your likeness or name will appear
- Whether it can be reused, resold, or altered
- The time frame for usage rights
- The compensation you'll receive

A strong clause to include is:

"Artist retains all rights of publicity, including name, likeness, image, and voice, unless otherwise agreed in writing."

Avoid vague or overly broad language such as "all media rights" or "in perpetuity" unless you are being fairly compensated and fully understand the implications. Your brand is part of your legacy, and contracts are essential to preserving both.

In some cases, protecting your name and likeness extends beyond the page; it becomes a public act of reputation defense, particularly in industries where visibility and identity are constantly monetized.

• Protecting Reputation Against Defamation

In 2025, Drake expanded a lawsuit against Universal Music Group, claiming the company made false public statements during the Super Bowl period that damaged his reputation and disrupted key business deals (*Drake v. Universal Music Group*, pending litigation, 2025). The case focuses on defamation, tortious interference, and legal claims tied to protecting reputation and business opportunities. While traditional IP law protects songs and logos, this dispute highlights the increasing need for artists to defend their name, image, and brand reputation as critical assets. The case remains pending, reflecting a legal shift where an artist's identity is as important to protect as the work they produce.

>> Artist Takeaway: Your brand extends beyond your work to your name and reputation. Strong contracts, non-disparagement clauses, and vigilant reputation monitoring are essential tools for protecting artistic legacy.

5.2 Licensing for Profit

Licensing lets artists turn their passion into profit while keeping creative control. Whether it is art, music, photos, or digital design, smart licensing helps you shape how your work is used and get paid for it. Success comes from clear agreements, understanding royalties, and navigating contracts with care.

Exclusive vs. Non-Exclusive

Before you license your work, it is essential to understand the difference between exclusive and non-exclusive rights. Your decision will influence how widely your work is distributed, the level of control you retain, and how much you may earn.

Licensing in Settlements

When someone uses your work without permission, you don't always have to fight it out in court. Sometimes, offering a license turns conflict into collaboration and gets you paid in the process.

(For examples of how licensing is used in IP settlement contexts, refer to 6.2 Cease-and-Desist.)

Royalty Agreements

Most revenue from licensing comes through royalty agreements, the financial engine behind many creative careers. A royalty is a recurring payment made to you, the rights holder, based on how often your licensed work is sold, used, or distributed. Instead of a one-time fee, you continue earning as your work generates value.

Whether it is a song streamed, a design printed, or a photo published, royalties compensate you in proportion to your work's reach. They reward not just the act of creating, but the strategy of licensing wisely.

1. Royalty Structures

Various methods may be employed to structure royalty payments within licensing agreements:

- Flat Fee (One-Time Payment) – An upfront sum exchanged for a license, often found in exclusive arrangements
- Revenue Share (Percentage-Based Royalty) – You receive a percentage of sales linked to your creation
- Minimum Guarantee Plus Royalties – A licensee pays a guaranteed base amount alongside royalties after sales surpass a certain threshold

Example: A musician licenses a song for a film, which earns an upfront fee plus 5% of sales, bringing in both instant and long-term income as the film gains traction.

2. Negotiating Royalty Rates

Royalty rates depend on industry standards, market demand, exclusivity, and the type of work. The Music Modernization Act (2018) changed how songwriters and rights holders are paid, introducing a centralized licensing system and standardizing streaming royalties. This has led to clearer benchmarks across the industry. Here are a few typical examples:

Industry	Typical Royalty Rate
Art Licensing (prints, merchandise)	5%-12% of retail price
Music Licensing (streaming, film)	10%-50% of revenue
Book Publishing (illustrations, covers)	8%-15% of book sales
Stock Photography & Digital Art	15%-50% of downloads

To ensure fairness and transparency, build clarity into your agreements:

- Payment schedule – Outline when you'll receive royalties, monthly, quarterly, or otherwise, so your income flows on a predictable rhythm
- Audit rights – Make sure you have the right to review sales reports, so you can verify that what's reported matches what's earned
- Territorial rights – Define where your work can be sold and where your royalties apply, whether locally or worldwide
- Expiration and renewal – Set clear terms for how long the agreement lasts and how it can be renewed, so you are not caught off guard

International Licensing

Licensing across countries can feel like navigating a maze of different IP laws, tax rules, and cultural norms.

1. Global Licensing Laws

Managing copyright internationally means knowing key differences across major markets:

Region	Key Legal Note	What Artists Should Do
United States	Copyright lasts for the creator's life + 70 years.	Understand long-term rights and plan for estate and legacy management.
European Union	Enforces strict digital copyright standards.	Ensure digital use complies with EU regulations.
China & India	Local registration is often required to enforce rights.	Register your work locally before distributing or licensing.

Best Practices for International Licensing:

Strategy	Why it Matters
Work with local legal pros	Understanding of regional IP laws.
Use standardized contracts	Ensures legal clarity and global recognition.
Register IP in each licensing region	Strengthens ability to enforce rights abroad.

2. Foreign Royalties & Taxes

Artists earning international royalties may face foreign taxes, but treaties like the U.S.–Canada agreement help reduce rates and avoid double taxation (U.S. Department of the Treasury & Government of Canada, 1980).

3. Currency Risk Management

When engaging in international licensing contracts, be sure to specify:

- Payments are made in reliable currencies (such as USD or EUR)
- Terms addressing exchange rates to navigate the unpredictable tides of currency fluctuations

Creative Control & Moral Rights

Many countries grant artists "moral rights" to credit and control their work. In the U.S., protections are limited, but you can add clauses to control use and edits.

** Artist Tip: If you're licensing your work, include a clause requiring approval for edits. It helps protect your creative integrity and reputation.

5.3 Work-for-Hire & Commissions

For independent artists, ownership matters, especially with commissions. In the U.S., clients don't automatically own the work; rights usually stay with the artist unless a contract states otherwise.

Who Owns Commissioned Work

Unless it's a true work-for-hire or rights are signed over, you still own what you create, even if you are paid. Always read contracts carefully to know when you are giving up ownership.

Example: A screenwriter hired to write a script still owns the script unless the contract specifies work-for-hire or assigns the copyright to it. Without clear terms, the production company must get permission to use or adapt it.

1. Work-for-Hire vs. Commissions

Category	Work-for-Hire	Commissioned Work
Ownership	Employer or client owns the copyright from the start.	Artist retains copyright unless explicitly transferred in writing.
Rights	Artist has no reuse or reproduction rights unless allowed by contract.	Artist retains reuse and licensing rights unless transferred.
Payment	Flat fee or salary under employment or contract.	Project-based pay; copyright does not automatically transfer.
Revisions	Client controls edits and final outcome.	Depends on contract; artist retains more creative control if rights are not transferred.

Remember: A work-for-hire must be in writing to be valid. Without a contract, the artist keeps the copyright. Freelancers should use licensing agreements when clients need usage rights but not full ownership.

2. Copyright by Creative Field

- Illustrators and Graphic Designers – Companies prefer work-for-hire, but freelancers can negotiate to retain rights and credit
- Photographers – Without a written agreement, clients don't own the copyright to commissioned photos
- Musicians and Composers – Scores for ads or films often default to work-for-hire; seek royalty agreements for ongoing income

Example: Under a work-for-hire agreement, a fashion brand owns the design; without the agreement, the illustrator retains copyright and reuse rights.

Independent Artist Tips

Independent artists should negotiate contracts that protect their work and pay, starting with clear, strategic terms like the ones below:

- Request a Deposit – Secure at least 50% upfront to protect against nonpayment
- Define Usage Terms – Specify context, medium, and duration
- Adjust for Ownership Transfers – Raise rates if granting full ownership
- Avoid Broad Work-for-Hire Contracts – Use precise licensing with renewal options to maintain long-term control

Example: A freelance photographer should license images for limited use. Scan the following for a sample Freelance Contract:

Freelance Contract

Protecting Against Misuse

As a creator, you often confront the realities of unauthorized use, unreciprocated services, or appropriated designs. Grasping your legal rights empowers you to defend your expressions and affirm your copyright ownership.

1. Handling Unauthorized Use

When you discover someone misusing your work without your consent, consider these proactive measures:

- Cease-and-Desist Letter: (See 6.2 Cease-and-Desist for a detailed explanation)
- *Digital Millennium Copyright Act* Takedown Notice: (See 6.1 Identifying IP Violations for more information)
- Copyright Infringement Lawsuit: If informal efforts fail, you may need to pursue legal action to recover damages. In the U.S., required damages are only available for registered works

2. Preventing Non-Payment

To protect against nonpayment, build these into your contracts:

- Kill Fee – Guarantees partial payment if a project is canceled
- Late Payment Penalties – Adds interest or fees to overdue invoices
- Watermarked Previews – Share low-res samples until full payment is received (see 7.3 for more on Watermarks).

Prince Appropriation Case

Richard Prince, known for his controversial "appropriation art," faced renewed legal challenges for using copyrighted Instagram screenshots in his series, which sold for over $100,000 without the original photographers' consent (*Graham v. Prince,* 2024). Although Prince claimed his edits constituted fair use, a federal judge ruled against him, finding that minimal changes did not sufficiently transform the original works. The case underscores that even when artistic intent is present, courts may not see a clear departure from the original.

>> Artist Takeaway: The case highlights a critical lesson: “Transformative” isn’t automatic. Always secure permission when using third-party content, and protect your work through clear contracts that define ownership.

Secure the Deal, Protect the Dream

Contracts are more than paperwork; they protect your creativity and turn it into ownership and opportunity. Draft clear terms, defend your rights early, and ensure that every collaboration respects your work. If those rights are violated, enforcement tools help you respond.

Contracts Toolkit

Licensing Checklist

Music Royalty Agreement

Work-for-Hire Agreement

NDA Cheatsheet

Contract Red Flags 🏳

1. "In Perpetuity" with No End Date

Gives away lifetime rights without future pay.
Fix: Set a time limit or review period.

2. Work-for-Hire with Low Pay

You lose copyright forever.
Fix: License instead or raise your fee.

3. Vague Usage Rights

"Any media" often means unlimited use beyond what you agreed to.
Fix: Define exactly where, how, and for how long they can use the work.

4. No Termination Clause

You could be stuck in a bad deal.
Fix: Add terms for ending the contract, especially for nonpayment or delays.

5. Broad Non-Compete

Could block you from other gigs.
Fix: Limit by time, location, or industry.

6. Payment on Delivery (No Late Fee)

You deliver the work, but payment stalls.
Fix: Add payment deadlines and late penalties.

7. Assignment of Rights

They can resell or sublicense your work without you.
Fix: Add approval rights or profit-sharing terms.

Infringement

Defend Your Work

6.1 Identifying IP Violations

Intellectual property infringement can lead to stress and financial loss. The illegal use of artistic works has become alarmingly frequent in our digital world. Artwork, photographs, music, and digital expressions can be replicated, shared, and sold without the artist's approval.

Learning to identify and address IP violations and incursions is essential. This section examines how to spot unauthorized use of your work, what actions to take when you uncover a violation, and how social media platforms manage IP complaints.

Spotting Unauthorized Use

As your work travels through the digital world, so does the risk of it being copied, reposted, or commercialized without your consent. Infringement can take many forms. Some are blatant, while others are harder to trace.

You might come across:

- A shared post that strips away your name or credit
- A sound clip lifted and layered into someone else's project
- A product sold online using your artwork, without your knowledge, permission, or payment

For years, many artists have relied on manual discovery, stumbling upon unauthorized uses while browsing, or hearing about them through supportive followers. While community awareness is still valuable, the scope of digital infringement today requires more than just chance encounters.

Fortunately, we now have access to various digital tools designed to help detect and track misuse. These technologies offer:

- Visual and audio detection of copied content
- Alerts and monitoring systems that scan the internet for your work
- Dashboards and filing tools embedded within major platforms

You don't need to master every system, but becoming familiar with even a few can dramatically reduce your response time, protect your rights, and ease the emotional toll of enforcement. These platforms support proactive control. They help you stay informed, respond efficiently, and safeguard longevity and visibility.

Once you've identified unauthorized use, the next step is knowing how to respond, starting with documentation.

What to Do if Infringed

If you discover your artistic work is being used without consent, you have several legal and informal options. Your response should match the seriousness of the infringement, the platform involved, and any financial repercussions. If your work is being used without permission, here's how to respond, starting with solid documentation.

Step 1: Gather Evidence

Before taking action, it's crucial to compile proof of the unauthorized use. This should include:

- Screenshots of the infringing material, with timestamps and URLs
- Side-by-side comparisons of your original work alongside the infringing content
- Records of purchases if your work is being sold without permission

If the situation escalates to legal proceedings, comprehensive documentation will bolster your case.

Step 2: Send a Cease-and-Desist

Cease-and-Desist Letter – (For template language and detailed usage instructions, refer to 6.2 Cease-and-Desist.)

Step 3: DMCA Takedown

Most major platforms, such as YouTube, Facebook, and Instagram, offer built-in tools allowing you to report copyright infringement and request the removal of unauthorized content. They generally operate under the Digital Millennium Copyright Act (DMCA), governing online takedown requests in the United States.

A basic DMCA notice typically includes:

- Proof of ownership and your contact information
- A link to the infringing content
- A good-faith statement that the use is unauthorized

(For a detailed breakdown of this process, refer to 6.2, and the Infringement Toolkit for a sample DMCA Takedown Request.)

** Artist Tip: The DMCA is a fast tool, but it has limits.

What it can do:

- Remove infringing copies from U.S.-based websites
- Prompt fast takedowns without needing a lawsuit
- Support your case if you later need to escalate legally

What it can't do:

- Stop others from reposting stolen content again elsewhere
- Guarantee success if the platform ignores or challenges your claim
- Protect your work across non-U.S. servers

Step 4: Consider Legal Action

If takedown requests or cease-and-desist letters (see 6.2) fail, legal action may be needed. Infringement lawsuits can bring statutory damages but require prior registration.

Beyond legal routes, many major platforms now offer built-in tools to help artists respond quickly and proactively to IP violations.

Social Media IP Complaints

As social media grows, so do IP violations. Users often share or alter art without consent. Most major platforms now offer tools to help artists protect their work more easily and proactively.

Tool	Function
Google Image Search	Upload an image or paste a URL to scan the internet for visual matches, helping you detect unauthorized reposts or uses of your artwork.
TinEye	Reverse image search that tracks where your image appears online and how it changes over time, ideal for identifying edited or repurposed versions.
Meta Rights Manager	Manage and protect your copyrighted content across Facebook and Instagram by detecting unlicensed uploads and claiming usage.
YouTube Content ID	Automatically scans uploaded videos for copyrighted audio or video, allowing creators to block, monetize, or track unauthorized use.
Manual Monitoring	Use Google alerts, keyword searches, and regular scans of marketplaces. Add watermarks or metadata to help trace and prove ownership.

1. Meta's Rights Manager

Facebook and Instagram offer an invaluable tool for artists called Rights Manager, designed specifically to help monitor and protect their content. With Rights Manager, you can:

- Upload reference images or video clips that serve as a blueprint for detecting unauthorized use
- Submit takedown requests for artwork or content that has been unlawfully copied, reposted, or repurposed
- Track unauthorized uses across the massive Meta social ecosystem

Artists must request access to Rights Manager through Meta's platform, but once granted, it serves as a powerful, ongoing defense against IP infringement.

2. YouTube Content ID

For musicians, videographers, and multimedia artists, YouTube's Content ID system serves as a vigilant digital guardian. It automatically scans uploaded videos and compares them against a vast database of registered works to detect unauthorized use. When a match is found, there are several enforcement options:

- Block the infringing video entirely
- Monetize the video by claiming ad revenue associated with the unauthorized use
- Track ongoing uses of their content across YouTube

This automation helps manage large volumes of content, but it is not perfect. In cases involving fair use, licensing disputes, or mistaken claims, manual review is often required. This ensures artists can override algorithmic errors and retain control over how their work is handled and monetized on the platform.

3. Twitter & TikTok's Reporting

Twitter and TikTok maintain streamlined copyright complaint procedures, offering fast responses when violations occur.

- Twitter: After a complaint is confirmed, infringing posts can be removed within 24 to 48 hours
- TikTok: The platform automatically detects and removes unauthorized use of copyrighted music and provides easy-to-access reporting tools for visual and written content

Both platforms empower artists to file straightforward complaints, although providing clear proof of ownership remains essential for swift resolution.

While major platforms offer built-in protections, online infringement isn't limited to social media. This was especially true in the case of Australian artist Emily Wright.

Emily Wright Art Theft Case

In 2023, Australian artist Emily Wright, founder of Ahki Illustration, discovered that one of her original lino designs was being sold without authorization by a third-party seller on the online retail platform Temu. The unauthorized merchandise was listed for under $6, significantly undervaluing her work (Herald Sun, 2023).

Wright discovered the unauthorized use of her work during a routine Google search, highlighting the importance of artists monitoring for online infringement. She reported the violation through Temu's IP claims process, prompting swift removal. Beyond her case, she flagged additional infringements and helped other artists protect their work.

>> Artist Takeaway: Art theft is real and widespread online. Stay alert, make use of reporting tools when needed, and support fellow artists to protect your rights.

You just found someone using your work without permission... Don't Panic!

Crisis Response Checklist

Secure Access

- ☐ Backup your files (cloud + hard drive)
- ☐ List key passwords and platform logins
- ☐ Name a trusted contact for emergencies

Gather Critical Documents

- ☐ Copyrights, trademarks, and contracts
- ☐ Licensing and royalty agreements
- ☐ IP clause in your will or trust

Protect Your Brand

- ☐ Register the key works before publishing
- ☐ Add licensing terms to your website
- ☐ Keep a DMCA takedown template ready

Prepare to Communicate

- ☐ Draft an emergency message for clients
- ☐ Set up auto-responses if needed
- ☐ Identify someone who can speak on your behalf

Create a Recovery Plan

- ☐ Build a "crisis folder" with your essentials
- ☐ Store it where your team or family can access it
- ☐ Review it every 6 months

Artist Takeaway: Crises don't wait. Prep now so your legacy and income stay protected, no matter what.

6.2 Cease-and-Desist & Legal Options

After discovering that your intellectual property has been used without permission, the next step is to enforce your rights. If you're unsure how to identify infringement or gather documentation (refer to subsection 6.1), for tools and strategies. One of the most common initial steps is sending a cease-and-desist letter, which formally demands that the infringer immediately stop using the work.

Sadly, not every infringer will comply. If a cease-and-desist letter is ignored, further legal action, including litigation, may be necessary. This section outlines how to craft an effective cease-and-desist letter, what to do if it is disregarded, and when it's time to consider legal action.

What is a Cease-and-Desist Letter

A cease-and-desist letter is a formal notice alerting infringers that they are violating your rights, typically by using your work without permission. It puts the violators on notice and gives them a chance to stop before legal action is pursued.

Drafting a Cease-and-Desist Letter

Your letter should clearly state who you are, what rights you hold, how those rights are being violated, and what you expect the recipient to do. Keep it direct, professional, and ready to serve as evidence if the issue escalates.

What to Include

Identify your work, assert ownership, and explain how it was used without permission. Request removal, written confirmation, and set a response deadline (7–14 days). Include your contact info for follow-up.

Scan the following for a sample letter:

Cease-and-Desist Letter

If Ignored: Next Steps

When someone chooses to dismiss your initial outreach, it may be time to chart a new course. Here's how you can navigate the situation:

1. Send Second Formal Notice

If the other party remains silent after your first attempt, follow up with a second, more urgent cease-and-desist letter. This should:

- Reinforce your initial requests
- Clearly articulate the potential for legal consequences
- Highlight additional damages that have arisen since your first communication

2. Submit a DMCA Takedown

If the infringement takes place online, such as on a website, social platform, or marketplace, you may be able to request its removal through a DMCA takedown notice. (See 6.1 Identifying IP Violations for detailed instructions, templates, and links to platform-specific tools).

3. Consult an Attorney

If your informal approaches yield no results, consider enlisting the expertise of an intellectual property attorney. A lawyer can:

- Draft a formal legal demand letter from a firm, which often carries more authority
- Prepare you for possible litigation should the situation escalate

Legal Avenues After Infringement

If your DMCA Notice or Cease-and-Desist letter does not yield the desired results, you may have to explore additional options.

Licensing & Settlement

(Refer to Subsection 5.2 Licensing for Profit)

Legal Action

If attempts at negotiation are unsuccessful, taking legal action might be necessary. In the United States, compensation for unauthorized use of your work is only available for registered copyrights, with potential damages varying from $750 to $150,000 per instance. Courts also have the authority to issue orders that compel infringers to cease their unlawful actions.

Financial Recovery Options

1. When to Consider a Lawsuit

You might consider litigation when:

- The infringement leads to measurable financial harm (such as reduced sales or damaged reputation)
- Your works have been duplicated or commercially exploited without your consent
- The infringer ignores repeated notices and demands for removal

2. What Options are Available

In a lawsuit, you may pursue:

- Actual damages (losses directly associated with the infringement)
- Statutory damages (up to $150,000 for each intentional infringement as outlined in 17 U.S.C. § 504)
- Injunctions to stop ongoing violations

3. Federal vs. Small Claims Court

- Federal Court - Essential for significant cases with large financial implications
- Copyright Claims Board (CCB) - An economical option for smaller disputes (those under $30,000)

• Blurred Lines Case Study

In 2013, Robin Thicke and Pharrell Williams were sued by Marvin Gaye's estate, which claimed their hit "Blurred Lines" copied the style, groove, and overall feel of Gaye's 1977 song "Got to Give It Up." After receiving and ignoring a cease-and-desist letter, the dispute escalated to a high-profile trial, where music experts compared rhythm, melody, bass lines, and the intangible "vibe" of both songs (*Williams v. Gaye, 2018*). (See the Infringement Toolkit for the records at issue.)

The jury ultimately sided with the Gaye estate, awarding the estate five million in damages and setting a controversial precedent: even emotional tone, stylistic similarity, and general atmosphere can lead to infringement liability. This decision reshaped how courts and artists view inspiration, especially when the original work holds iconic cultural status.

>> Artist Takeaway

- Don't assume "inspiration" is risk-free
- Courts may view stylistic borrowing as infringement, especially with well-known works
- Even emotional tone or artistic feel can raise legal issues
- Legal exposure isn't limited to melodies or lyrics; style and atmosphere matter too

Comparing Cases: Inspiration vs. Imitation

While Blurred Lines set a precedent by favoring the original artist's estate, more recent cases like Ed Sheeran v. Gaye Estate have pushed back on that trend.

In 2023, Sheeran successfully defended "Thinking Out Loud" against claims it copied Marvin Gaye's "Let's Get It On," with the court ruling the shared chord progression wasn't original enough to be protected. For full details. (See 2.3 Infringement & Fair Use.)

Blurred Lines focused on musical 'feel', but visual art has faced its fair use reckoning, as seen in the Warhol case.

● The Limits of Fair Use: "Warhol Estate"

In 2023, the U.S. Supreme Court issued a landmark ruling in *Andy Warhol Foundation v. Goldsmith (2023)* that reshaped how courts evaluate transformative use. Warhol had created a silkscreen portrait of Prince based on a photograph by Lynn Goldsmith. Although Warhol's artwork was visually altered, the Court found that it served a similar commercial purpose as Goldsmith's original photograph, concluding it was not protected under fair use (*In re Estate of Andy Warhol, 1995*).

This decision marked a major shift in fair use doctrine: transforming the appearance of a work is no longer enough. Courts now focus on whether the new work has a distinctly different purpose or message from the original. If both works target the same audience, serve a similar market function, or compete for licensing opportunities, even dramatic stylistic changes may not qualify for fair use protections.

>> Artist Takeaway

- Reused work must add new meaning or commentary, not a new look
- Fair use requires a clear transformation in purpose and message, especially for visual artists

6.3 Global IP Protection

In today's global scene, protecting your work stretches far beyond home turf. Knockoffs, piracy, and unauthorized use can emerge anywhere, often in countries with unfamiliar or less predictable legal systems. Understanding how international protections work is essential for staying ahead.

This section breaks down practical tools like the Madrid Protocol, major global copyright treaties, and strategies to help you safeguard your rights across borders.

Protecting Rights Abroad

Navigating the labyrinth of foreign legal systems can be daunting, as each country presents its enforcement practices, timelines, and levels of IP recognition. Yet despite these challenges, international treaties like the Madrid Protocol and local enforcement channels offer powerful tools to secure and defend your rights abroad.

With strategic planning, artists and brands can turn complex global systems into opportunities for broader protection.

1. Registering IP Abroad

While copyright springs to life the moment you create, trademarks and patents require the formal embrace of registration in each desired jurisdiction.

Copyright Protection:

- Copyright is born spontaneously under the Berne Convention (*Berne Convention for the Protection of Literary and Artistic Works*, 1886/1979), but taking the extra step to register in foreign territories can fortify your claims
- In places like China, India, and Brazil, local copyright registration is essential for ensuring your legal protection

Trademark and Patent Protection:

- Unique applications must be submitted for trademarks and patents in each country, unless a specific international treaty, such as the Madrid Protocol for trademarks, covers both (*Madrid Protocol*, 1989/1996)
- Overlooking registration in key markets allows counterfeiters to legally seize your creative identity

Example: Digital artists who sell prints worldwide only to discover their work is being exploited without consent by an overseas entity. Without local copyright registration, their avenues for recourse are significantly limited.

2. Monitoring Global Violations

It is vital for creators to vigilantly scout international landscapes for any unauthorized use of their masterpieces. Tools and strategies abound to assist in this endeavor:

- Google Reverse Image Search & TinEye – Keep tabs on global image usage

- Customs and Border Protection (CBP) Monitoring - Certain nations enable registered trademarks to be safeguarded at ports against counterfeiting
- Third-Party IP Protection Firms - Services like Red Points deploy automated defenses against piracy and counterfeiting

Example: Fashion Designers who trademark their brands in the U.S. may encounter counterfeit versions appearing on platforms like Alibaba in China. Monitoring tools can play a critical role in detecting and reporting these unauthorized listings.

3. Enforcing Rights Locally

Upon spotting an infringement, enforcement steps vary by country:

- Sending Cease-and-Desist Letters - Some jurisdictions require formal notice before legal action (see 6.2 Cease-and-Desist)
- Filing DMCA Takedowns on International Websites - Many platforms accept U.S. DMCA requests, though some require local procedures
- Legal Proceedings in Local Courts - Serious infringements may require engaging a local IP attorney

Example: A U.S. photographer finds her work marketed in Europe without permission. She may need to register the copyright in the EU before pursuing legal action.

Madrid Protocol Protection

For someone building a global brand, the Madrid Protocol enables trademark registration in multiple regions through one application via WIPO. (See the Infringement Toolkit for the registration form.)

1. Understanding the Madrid Protocol

The Madrid Protocol lets trademark owners seek protection in multiple countries through one centralized application (Madrid Protocol, 1989), streamlining filings, reducing legal costs, and simplifying renewals.

As of 2023, over 130 countries, including the US, EU, China, Japan, Australia, Canada, and Brazil, participate in the Madrid System.

○ Madrid Protocol Countries

Map adopted from WIPO

2. Madrid Registration Steps

1. Register Locally: First, register or apply for your trademark in your home country
2. File Internationally: Then file a single Madrid Protocol application through WIPO

3. Select Countries: Choose where you want protection
4. National Review: Each selected country will independently approve or reject your application
5. Renew & Enforce: Renew every 10 years to maintain rights across chosen countries

Example: Digital artists who trademark their brand in the U.S. can use the Madrid Protocol to expand protection across Europe and China for their NFTs.

Global Copyright Treaties

Imagine a world where your imagination holds the highest value, instantly shielded from infringement the moment it comes to life. In reality, copyright protection does arise automatically, but how it is recognized, enforced, and valued can vary dramatically across borders. Different nations weave a complex and sometimes conflicting web of rights, causing challenges for artists seeking to safeguard their work internationally.

1. The Berne Convention

The Berne Convention for the Protection of Literary and Artistic Works is a treaty first signed in 1886 and stands as a vital landmark in the landscape of global copyright, establishing the principle that creative works deserve automatic protection without the need for formal registration. Since its adoption, it has been embraced by 181 member nations, forming a powerful international framework for artists (Berne Convention, 1886/1979).

Key Provisions:

- Instantaneous Protection – Copyright arises the moment a work is created, with no registration required in any Berne member country
- Minimum Protection Duration – Rights are guaranteed for at least 50 years after the author's death, with many countries extending that period to 70 years or more, ensuring a lasting legacy

- Moral Rights – Artists maintain the right to be credited for their work and to protect its integrity against distortion or misrepresentation, even if they transfer economic rights

Example: An American painter whose work is copied in France can assert rights and seek remedies under the Berne Convention's shared protections.

2. The TRIPS Agreement

The TRIPS Agreement, established under the World Trade Organization, sets the stage for stronger, more uniform enforcement of intellectual property rights worldwide. It creates minimum standards for protection across copyrights, trademarks, patents, and trade secrets, influencing how nations structure and enforce their IP laws (*Agreement on Trade-Related Aspects of Intellectual Property Rights* [TRIPS], 1994).

Key Provisions:

- Enforces adherence to the Berne Convention as the gold standard in copyright protection
- Strengthens the fabric of intellectual property rights through the lens of international trade laws
- Establishes pathways for resolving disputes that cross national boundaries

3. The Universal Copyright Convention

The Universal Copyright Convention (UCC) was adopted in 1952 as an alternative treaty to the Berne Convention for countries that didn't initially join Berne. Although it lacks the same global resonance as Berne, some countries lean on the UCC for copyright security (*Universal Copyright Convention* [UCC], 1952/1971).

Example: A Canadian filmmaker seeking protection in Taiwan would rely on the Universal Copyright Convention (UCC), as Taiwan is not part of the Berne Convention.

Disney Copyright Case (China)

Disney has faced ongoing copyright challenges in China, including unauthorized use of its characters, films, and trademarks ("Disney Wins 'Cars' Copyright Suit in China," 2016). Trademark squatting and counterfeit goods threatened both revenue and brand value. In response, Disney used the Madrid Protocol to strengthen its trademarks, collaborated with authorities to target counterfeiters, and pursued legal action, setting important precedents for international IP enforcement.

>> Artist Takeaway: Building a global brand demands early action. Even giant corporations like Disney face trademark squatting and counterfeiting abroad. Protect your work internationally, use tools like the Madrid Protocol, and stay alert; a strong IP portfolio shields your brand from dilution and loss.

Defend What You Create

Protecting your work requires more than reacting; it means anticipating risks, acting strategically, and defending your rights across industries and borders. From cease-and-desist letters to global trademarks, artists must be their own first line of defense, turning ownership into real, enforceable power.

Infringement Toolkit

How to Track IP Work

Blurred Lines & Got to Give it Up records
(*Willams vs. Gaye, 2018*)
Used under fair use for educational and commentary purposes.

DMCA Takedown Notice

Madrid Protocol Guide

Digital IP

NFTs, AI & Art

7.1 NFTs & Blockchain

The rise of non-fungible tokens (NFTs) has transformed the way artists, musicians, and digital creators earn from and protect their masterpieces. By harnessing the power of blockchain technology, NFTs present a novel avenue for affirming ownership, tracing a creation's journey, and upholding licensing terms. Yet, this vibrant landscape also unveils significant legal challenges, particularly in intellectual property and copyright matters.

In this section, we will explore the essence of NFTs, their impact on intellectual property rights, the role of smart contracts in NFT licensing, and the complex legal tapestry of NFTs concerning copyright law.

NFTs & IP Rights

1. Understanding NFTs

An NFT is a unique digital asset on a blockchain, unlike interchangeable cryptocurrencies. Its distinctiveness makes it ideal for verifying the authenticity of digital art, music, and other artworks.

NFTs in Creative Sectors

NFTs serve as digital proofs of ownership and authenticity. When an artist creates an NFT, it is recorded on a blockchain, establishing a permanent trail that:

- Confirms the artist's identity
- Monitors all future transactions and transfers
- Enables automatic royalty payments via NFT code

2. NFTs & IP Issues

While NFTs establish token ownership, the blockchain record of a digital asset, they do not automatically transfer copyright or intellectual property rights to the buyer. Ownership of the token is distinct from ownership of the underlying work. Unless explicitly stated through a license or rights transfer, the original creator retains full legal control over reproduction, distribution, and modification.

Understanding this distinction is critical for those seeking to protect their work and collectors hoping to use it beyond display. See the following diagram:

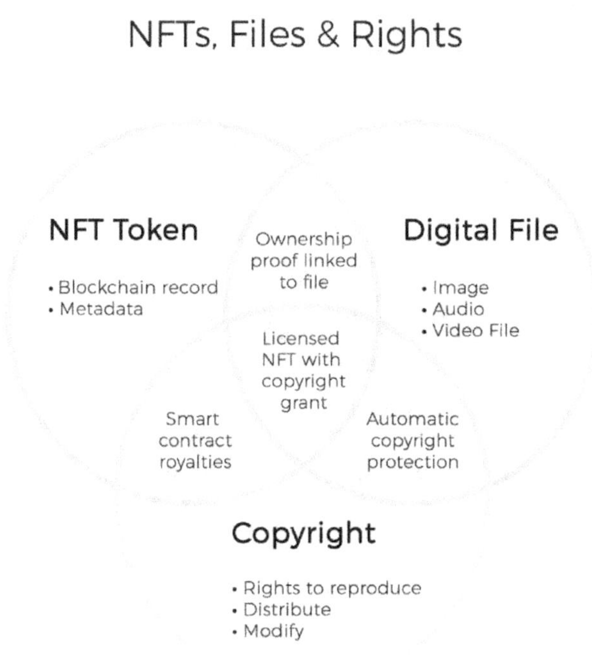

Example: A digital artist mints an NFT of his painting but retains the copyright, meaning buyers own the NFT but cannot legally reproduce, sell, or modify the artwork without his permission.

Smart Contracts

A key feature of NFTs is smart contracts, which automate licensing and royalty payments through blockchain, removing the need for intermediaries.

1. Smart Contracts in NFT Licensing

A smart contract is a piece of code embedded within an NFT that outlines the terms of its use, resale, or distribution. Smart contracts empower:

- Automated royalty payments
- Usage restrictions
- Transfer conditions

Example: An NFT developer sets a 10% royalty, and when the piece resells for $10,000, the smart contract automatically sends $1,000 to the artist. This process is handled through smart contract code, as shown in the example below.

Smart Contract 10% Royalty Code

```
// SPDX-License-Identifier: MIT
pragma solidity ^0.8.0;

import "@openzeppelin/contracts/token/ERC721/extensions/ERC721Royalty.sol";

contract LionArtNFT is ERC721Royalty {
  uint256 public nextTokenId;
  address public admin;

  constructor() ERC721("LionArt", "LION") {
    admin = msg.sender;
  }

  function mint(address to, string memory uri) external {
    require(msg.sender == admin, "Only admin can mint");
    uint256 tokenId = nextTokenId;
    _safeMint(to, tokenId);
    _setTokenURI(tokenId, uri);
    _setTokenRoyalty(tokenId, admin, 1000); // 1000 basis points = 10%
    nextTokenId++;
  }
}
```

2. Licensing Models for NFTs

Traditional License:

An NFT can come with a copyright license that specifies or curtails certain rights for the buyer. (See NFT License Template in Digital IP Toolkit.)

- Personal Use License: The NFT holder may display the artwork but not reproduce it for profit
- Commercial License: The NFT holder can create and sell merchandise or derivative works based on the NFT
- Exclusive vs. Non-Exclusive License: Some artists provide NFTs with exclusive rights, granting full authority to the buyer

Creative Commons & Open Licenses:

Certain NFT initiatives adopt Creative Commons (CC0) licenses, placing works in the public domain. This framework allows anyone to use, modify, and share the content freely.

For instance, the Nouns NFT (*Nouns DAO*, 2024) project operates under a CC0 license, granting individuals the freedom to develop derivative works openly.

3. Challenges with Smart Contracts

Smart contracts promise our world efficiency and transparency, yet they often struggle to earn legal recognition across various jurisdictions.

- A simple error in a smart contract can lead to devastating financial consequences
- Not every legal complication can be resolved through blockchain technology; at times, we must rely on traditional legal avenues
- NFT marketplaces may enforce their policies, which can conflict with the original terms of smart contracts

Imagine this: A developer embeds a royalty clause in an NFT, but a new marketplace permits zero-royalty transactions, undermining the creator's sincere intention.

Challenges with NFTs and Copyright

Despite their intriguing benefits, NFTs introduce a web of legal uncertainties, particularly in copyright enforcement, fair use, and digital rights management.

1. Unauthorized NFT Minting

A significant barrier in the NFT arena is copyright infringement, where individuals mint NFTs of artwork that isn't theirs.

Example of Unauthorized NFT Sales

- A digital artist discovers that her artwork has been minted as an NFT on OpenSea without approval
- The NFT minter enjoys profits from these sales while the original artist sees none
- The artist faces a complex journey to remove the unauthorized NFT

While some NFT platforms provide copyright reporting tools, the challenge of consistent enforcement looms large.

2. International Enforcement

Given the decentralized nature of NFTs, a multitude of jurisdictional complications arise:

- Which nation's copyright laws apply?
- Who takes responsibility for enforcing copyright violations in today's interconnected digital landscape?
- How do courts interpret NFT ownership in terms of copyright?

Legal experts foresee the establishment of cohesive global regulations that will delineate NFT copyright.

3. Theft & Fraud in NFT Marketplaces

The rise of scams and fraudulent NFT projects casts a shadow over both developers and collectors:

- Counterfeit NFTs: Scammers develop and sell NFTs of artwork they do not own
- Rug pulls: NFT projects promise returns but vanish after the sale
- Imitation digital assets: Unauthorized reproductions flood secondary marketplaces

Platforms like OpenSea, Rarible, and Foundation are implementing IP verification measures, though the efficacy of these initiatives remains a work in progress.

● MetaBirkins NFT Lawsuit

In 2021, artist Mason Rothschild launched MetaBirkins, NFTs inspired by Hermès' Birkin bags, drawing attention and a swift lawsuit. Hermès sued for trademark infringement, claiming Rothschild exploited the Birkin brand without permission (*Hermès v. Rothschild, 2023*).

The court ruled in favor of Hermès, confirming that trademark protections apply to NFTs as they do to physical goods. This landmark decision strengthened luxury brand rights in digital spaces and affirmed that NFTs are subject to traditional IP laws.

>> Artist Takeaway: NFTs don't override trademark or copyright obligations, and using brand names or designs without permission can lead to legal action. Artists should assess intellectual property risks before launching NFTs tied to existing brands or properties.

7.2 AI-Generated Art & Copyright

The rapid rise of artificial intelligence (AI) is transforming industries and raising critical questions about copyright, authorship, and ownership. As AI-generated art, music, and literature become more common, they challenge laws designed for humans.

The U.S. Copyright Office's 2025 report, *Copyright and Artificial Intelligence: Part II – Copyrightability,* reaffirms that copyright protects only works created by humans, regardless of how advanced the technology becomes (U.S. Copyright Office, 2025). This section explores how AI-generated works are challenging copyright law, particularly as algorithms are used to produce art, music, and writing. These developments raise new questions about authorship and originality under a legal system built for humans. At the center of this evolving debate are shifting policies and real-world disputes that are beginning to shape how copyright law responds to machine-generated content.

Who Owns AI-Generated Art

Traditionally, copyright law has centered on human authorship, offering protection to those who craft original works. The rise of AI-generated content complicates this narrative, as many works emerge without direct human involvement. The pressing inquiry today is: Can AI-generated art be copyrighted, and if so, who deserves the credit?

1. Requirement of Human Authorship

Most global copyright laws, including those in the U.S., EU, and Canada, require human authorship. The U.S. Copyright Office states, "Copyright law only protects works created by human authors. AI-generated works lacking human authorship do not qualify for copyright protection" (U.S. Copyright Office, 2023).

● The Monkey Selfie Ruling

In (*Naruto v. Slater, 2018*), a macaque took a selfie using a photographer's camera, prompting a legal battle over copyright ownership. The court ultimately ruled that animals cannot hold copyrights, reinforcing that only human works qualify for protection. This principle is now central to ongoing debates about AI-generated content. (See the "Monkey Selfie" in the Digital IP Toolkit.)

>> Artist Takeaway: Even animals are not eligible for copyright protection; it is not exclusive to machines and algorithms.

2. Ownership Issue

Who owns AI-generated work depends on how it is crafted:

- AI as a tool – If an artist guides the process, adds input, and makes choices, he may hold the copyright
- Fully autonomous AI – If the AI produces the work without human input, most countries don't recognize any copyright
- Corporate-owned AI – Companies that build AI systems may claim rights through software licenses

Example: In 2018, Christie's sold *Portrait of Edmond de Belamy*, created by a neural network, for $432,500. Since no human authored it directly, the legal ownership remains unclear (Kinsella, 2018). (See Portrait of Edmond de Belamy in the Digital IP Toolkit.)

3. Global Perspectives on AI & Copyright

Countries around the world have taken diverse and evolving stances on AI-generated works. The absence of a unified global perspective has intensified the growing debates around authorship, ownership, and the future of intellectual property law in the age of artificial intelligence. Different regions are shaping unique policies that artists must navigate carefully.

Country	Policy Summary
United States	Copyright requires human authorship. AI-generated works are denied protection.
United Kingdom	AI-created works can be protected, but ownership belongs to the person who arranged the AI's creation.
China	AI-generated content may qualify if substantial human input is involved.
European Union	No explicit laws; human authorship is generally required.

Trademarking & Copyrighting AI Work

1. Copyright for AI-Generated Creations

Works designed solely by autonomous AI generally aren't eligible for copyright. However, if a human plays a meaningful role, she may still claim authorship.

Example: In 2023, the U.S. Copyright Office denied protection for the AI-generated visuals in *Zarya of the Dawn*, granting copyright only to the human-created elements like the story and layout (U.S. Copyright Office, 2023).

2. Trademarking AI-Produced Content

In contrast to copyright, trademarks can effectively shield AI-generated logos, names, or slogans, provided they adhere to the legal criteria for distinctiveness.

Challenges with AI-Generated Trademarks:

- Issues of originality – AI-crafted logos may struggle to meet the standards of uniqueness required for trademark protection
- Complexities of ownership – When multiple people/entities produce similar AI-generated logos, pinpointing ownership can become a daunting task

- Potential trademark disputes – AI might inadvertently craft logos that closely resemble existing trademarks, leading to possible legal complications

One of the most high-profile legal battles over AI and copyright came in 2023, when Getty Images took direct aim at Stability AI.

Getty Images v. Stability AI

In 2023, Getty Images sued Stability AI for training Stable Diffusion on millions of its copyrighted images without permission, calling it clear infringement. Stability AI argued the outputs are "transformative" and protected as fair use (*Getty Images v. Stability AI,* 2023).

The case raises critical questions

- Can AI legally train on copyrighted material without licensing it?
- Who is responsible when AI-generated content infringes rights?
- Should new laws be enacted to govern how AI interacts with intellectual property?

>> Artist Takeaway: The Getty v. Stability AI case could redefine AI art rights. A win for Getty may tighten licensing rules, while a win for Stability could broaden fair use. Either outcome will shape the future of artistic rights in the AI age.

Moral Rights & Ethics of Attribution

As AI-generated art grows, so do ethical concerns: Who gets credit, and can AI distort an artist's vision? While U.S. moral rights are limited, many countries offer stronger protections for attribution and integrity, especially important when AI reuses human work without consent. Even if not legally required, crediting artists and using attribution clauses in contracts respects ownership and promotes transparency.

7.3 Selling & Protecting Art Online

The internet gives artists powerful platforms to showcase and sell their work, but it also brings risks like infringement, unauthorized use, and art theft. To thrive online, artists must know how to protect their rights, use digital safeguards, and take action through tools like DMCA takedowns.

E-commerce and Social Media Protection

Navigating the sale of artwork online, be it digital or physical, requires a keen awareness of copyright safeguards and the vulnerabilities associated with major e-commerce and social media platforms.

1. Copyrighting for Digital Artists

Your original work is protected by copyright from the moment of creation. (For more on how this applies to licensing, selling, and ownership, refer to 5.2 Licensing for Profit.)

Selling Art on Marketplaces - Platforms such as Etsy, Redbubble, and similar print-on-demand services empower artists to share digital designs, prints, and merchandise. Unfortunately, these arenas are breeding grounds for art theft, where rogue sellers:

- Download artwork and re-upload it for personal gain
- Print unauthorized artwork on items like T-shirts and phone cases
- Produce imitations of original designs

Social media and Copyright - While social media provides a stage for artists to broadcast their work, it also renders art susceptible to:

- Unauthorized shares from users who do not credit the original author
- Fake profiles posing as artists to market counterfeit work
- Algorithm-driven impersonations, where AI-generated images mimic popular styles

Though these platforms extend tools for copyright defense, their enforcement often resembles a slow-moving ship in turbulent waters.

2. Protecting Copyright on Marketplaces

Artists can take proactive measures to shield their work on e-commerce and social media platforms through the following strategies:

- Register Copyrights for Key Works – Registering significant pieces with the U.S. Copyright Office strengthens your legal standing in infringement disputes
- Monitor Marketplaces for Unauthorized Listings – Regularly scour platforms like Etsy and Redbubble for unlicensed reproductions of your work
- Enable Rights Management Tools on Social Media – Tools like Meta's Rights Manager assist in curbing unauthorized use of copyrighted work on Facebook and Instagram

(For guidance on DMCA takedowns, cease-and-desist letters, and detecting infringement online, refer to subsections 6.1 and 6.2.)

Digital Watermarks & Metadata

To deter unauthorized downloads and reproductions, artists can utilize digital watermarks and metadata embedding.

1. Digital Watermarks

A digital watermark is an ethereal emblem, signature, or symbol woven into an image, rendering it challenging to steal without compromising the original work.

Types of Watermarks

- Visible Watermarks – Typically positioned in a corner or superimposed on the image to signify ownership

- Invisible Watermarks – Embedded within the image file, identifiable using specialized software
- Dynamic Watermarks – Sophisticated markings that change when copied, enhancing the capacity for detection

Watermarking Best Practices:

- Place the watermark over essential areas to make removal a daunting task
- Utilize a semi-transparent watermark that remains perceptible without overshadowing the artwork
- Maintain a high-resolution version of your art absent of a watermark for potential licensing opportunities

Example: A freelance illustrator offering prints on Etsy strategically places a discreet watermark across image previews to discourage theft while ensuring the design remains discernible.

2. Metadata & Image Fingerprinting

Metadata is hidden information embedded in a digital file, such as the artist's name, creation date, copyright status, and usage terms, that helps protect your rights by linking your identity to the work in a traceable, verifiable way. Here's how metadata protects copyright:

- Serves as digital proof of ownership in disputes
- Enhances tracking and authenticity across platforms
- Can be paired with image fingerprinting tools, like Adobe's Content Authenticity Initiative, to assign a unique digital ID to each work

Many platforms strip metadata during uploads, so using external tools is key to preserving authorship records. For tools like TinEye, Google Reverse Image Search, and Rights Manager. (See 6.1 Identifying IP Violations.)

Example: A photographer embeds metadata and an invisible watermark in digital prints. If reposted without permission, this data confirms ownership and supports quick takedown requests.

Even with watermarks and metadata, enforcement often lags, especially on fast-moving platforms like Etsy.

• The Etsy Art Theft Case

In 2021, numerous independent artists on Etsy discovered that their original illustrations and designs were being unlawfully sold by unauthorized sellers (ATP Journal, 2022). Rogue sellers downloaded original artworks and marketed them on products like T-shirts, phone cases, and posters. Etsy's automated copyright system struggled to keep pace, failing to prevent repeated violations. Despite hundreds of DMCA takedown notices filed by affected artists, infringers continually re-uploaded stolen works under new listings.

In response, artists took a multi-pronged approach: filing DMCA takedowns not only on Etsy but also across platforms like Amazon, using reverse image searches to trace unauthorized sellers, and turning to social media, particularly Twitter, to publicly pressure Etsy into adopting stronger protective measures.

>> Artist Takeaway: Etsy's updates to seller verification and repeat infringement tools came after artist pushback. Protecting your work still requires vigilance, using watermarks, tracking misuse, and speaking out when platforms fall short.

As technology evolves, questions around creativity and ownership are just beginning; AI and blockchain are only the opening scene.

• Johansson v. OpenAI Case

In 2025, Scarlett Johansson challenged OpenAI after it released "Sky," a voice assistant whose tone closely resembled her own. Although Johansson had declined OpenAI's earlier request to license her voice, the final product still sounded strikingly similar. Her legal team responded with demands based on Right of Publicity and false endorsement concerns (Northeastern University, 2025; AP News, 2024).

>> Artist Takeaway: The case remains unresolved, but it highlights a growing frontier: artists must now defend their identity itself against unauthorized AI replication.

Owning Creativity in the Digital Age

As technology reshapes artistry, the tools artists use, from NFTs to AI, offer new opportunities but also demand new defenses. Ownership, authorship, and authenticity must be intentionally protected in the digital age. By understanding the legal frameworks emerging around blockchain, AI, and online marketplaces, today's artists can secure not just their work but their voice and future.

Digital IP Toolkit

AI Case Studies

NFT License Template

The famous "Monkey Selfie"
(*Naruto vs. Slater, 2018*)
Used under fair use for educational and commentary purposes.

Portrait of Edmond de Belammy was created by an AI algoritm (Kinsella, 2018)
Used under fair use for educational and commentary purposes.

Legacy

Protect Your IP Future

8.1 IP Portfolio Management

Managing your IP portfolio is about taking control of your legacy. Understanding copyrights, trademarks, and patents helps protect and grow your brand. These tools are not just legal strategies; they are creative fuel. Treating your IP as part of your business strategy opens doors to income, visibility, and long-term success.

This section guides you through the essentials of nurturing your IP over time, from tracking your rights to renewing registrations and exploring smart licensing opportunities. You will also discover a real-world case study of artists who turned their IP into a thriving brand by actively managing and protecting their assets. Strong IP management isn't just for big companies; it's a powerful step toward sustainability and ownership for an artistic career.

Tracking Copyrights, Trademarks & Patents

Managing your IP portfolio starts with the basics, keeping track of what you own and how it is protected. That protection starts with keeping your intellectual property organized. It might sound technical, but it's really about giving your imagination the care and structure it needs to grow.

Think of your IP portfolio as a living archive of your journey. Keeping it organized helps protect your rights and opens doors to future opportunities.

(If you want to go deeper, see subsections 2.2 for copyright registration, 3.2 for trademark steps, and 8.2 for tips on valuing your work.)

The following chart shows what to keep track of, where to store it, and how often to check in.

IP Portfolio Management Chart

IP Type	What to Track	Storage	Review Schedule
Copyrights	Original works, registration certificates, publication details, contracts, licenses.	Secure digital archive with metadata and timestamps.	Every 6–12 months, or before publishing or selling a new work.
Trademarks	Registered marks, renewals, licenses, monitoring reports.	Maintain a trademark tracker and archive legal documents.	Quarterly, or prior to launching new branding or products.
Patents	Filed patents, specifications/drawings, revenue logs, renewal status.	Use a docketing system or inventor's log (digital + physical).	Every 6 months, or before disclosure, licensing, or development steps.

** Artist Tip: Use calendar alerts, task reminders, and folder templates to automate reviews, stay organized, and reduce the risk of missing key deadlines or important filing requirements.

Valuing Your IP Assets

Once you've organized your IP, the next step is understanding its value, because what you've built could be worth more than you think.

1. Methods for Valuing IP

There are a few ways to put a price on your work, whether it is a copyright, trademark, or patent

Income-Based Valuation:

This method looks at how much income your IP generates now and in the future. Royalties and licensing fees help shape its value.

Example: A songwriter earning $50,000 annually in royalties can use that steady stream to estimate the worth of her copyright.

Market-Based Valuation:

Under this method, your IP is compared to similar works that have sold or been licensed. Past deals in your industry set useful benchmarks.

Example: A film script optioned by a studio for $200,000 reflects its market value based on comparable deals.

Cost-Based Valuation:

This focuses on what you have invested in developing the IP, such as development, legal, or branding costs.

Example: A patented painting technique that cost $10,000 to develop and register would need to generate more than $10,000 in income to justify its value.

Each method helps you understand and advocate for the real worth of your work.

2. Why IP Valuation Matters

Valuing your intellectual property is essential for making informed business decisions. It allows you to license your work fairly, negotiate with confidence, attract investors or funding partners, and plan your legacy with clarity.

Understanding the value of your intellectual property is key to both income and legal protection.

- Accurate valuation supports stronger claims in infringement disputes
- A well-organized IP portfolio boosts earning potential and legal leverage

IP Business Planning

With a clear picture of what your IP is worth, you can put it to work, turning protection into strategy and ownership into income.

1. IP-Centric Business Model

Your business strategy should shine a spotlight on your IP and articulate:

- Revenue streams (e.g., licensing, direct sales, royalties)
- Protective measures (copyrights, trademarks, patents)
- Marketing and branding tactics

Example: Revenue Models for IP-Based Businesses

2. Licensing and Monetization

Exclusive vs. Non-Exclusive Licensing

- An exclusive license grants full rights to one entity, often for a higher fee, while a non-exclusive license lets multiple parties use the work simultaneously

Royalties and Passive Income

- Percentage-based royalties offer steady, long-term income, while platforms like Patreon and NFTs have transformed how digital work is shared and monetized

Leveraging Digital Marketplaces

- Creative minds can market and protect their work through trusted platforms, turning ideas into lasting income

Disney's IP Portfolio Management

The Walt Disney Company possesses an immensely valuable intellectual property portfolio, encompassing beloved animated films, enchanting theme parks, iconic character trademarks, and a vast array of patents (Allan Gray Proprietary Limited, 2023).

How Disney Manages Its Portfolio:

- Strong Copyright Safeguards – Disney ensures all films, scripts, and characters are protected under U.S. copyright law
- Trademarking Iconic Symbols – Cherished icons such as Mickey Mouse and the Disney logo, along with popular franchises, are trademarked globally
- Innovative Patent Strategies for Theme Parks – Disney secures its advancements in ride technology and engaging experiences through patent protections
- Proactive IP Enforcement – Disney diligently oversees unauthorized usage and promptly initiates legal action against violators
- Merchandising and Licensing Revenue – Disney reaps billions annually from licensed products, streaming opportunities, and strategic collaborations

>> Artist Takeaway

- The enduring power of intellectual property ensures a steady revenue stream; for example, Mickey Mouse has stood as a profitable asset for nearly a hundred years
- Thoughtful licensing reinforces brand visibility across diverse sectors
- Strong legal defenses prevent brand dilution while enhancing market dominance

8.2 Estate Planning for Artists

Managing your IP while you are active is only part of the picture. Protecting it after you are gone is just as important. Without clear guidance, intellectual property can be divided unpredictably, diluted, or even forgotten.

This section highlights why estate planning is essential for protecting the long-term value and integrity of your work.

Key areas include:

- Exploring what happens to an artist's intellectual property after death
- Identifying beneficiaries and setting clear instructions for assets
- Understanding how trusts and wills safeguard artistic legacy and ensure a vision endures

Legacy Planning Steps

Legacy Goal: Plan Licensing & Management
Set posthumous licensing & protection strategies

↑

Implementation: Appoint an IP Executor
Choose someone skilled in handling creative assets

|

Preperation: Draft an IP Will or Trust
Define who inherits & manges your creative works

|

Foundation: Inventory & Update IP
Catalog all copyrights, trademarks, patents & licensing agreements

IP Rights After Death

When artists, writers, or musicians pass away, copyright law continues to protect their work for a set period, allowing it to generate income for their estate. How those rights are managed depends on whether the artist constructed an estate plan in advance.

• Bob Ross vs. Michael Jackson

Bob Ross, despite his warm public image, made estate planning missteps with lasting effects. He signed away rights to his name, image, and intellectual property to business partners during his lifetime. After his death, those rights remained with Bob Ross Inc., leaving his family with little control or benefit from how his likeness has been used in merchandise and licensing (Schwarz, 2021).

In contrast, Michael Jackson's estate demonstrates strategic, high-level IP planning. After he died in 2009, professional executors managed the estate with a clear focus on protecting and expanding his intellectual property. Through licensing, catalog sales, and brand management, the estate generated over $2 billion in a decade, preserving Jackson's legacy while controlling how his name, image, and music are shared with the world (Ryzik, 2019).

>> Artist Takeaway: Planning isn't just about who inherits your work; it's about protecting your identity, supporting your family, and preserving your vision. While artists like Ross lost control by not planning, those like Jackson show that strategic decisions can ensure your legacy continues to thrive on your terms.

Moral Rights After Death

Estate planning goes beyond finances; it protects your artistic intent and legacy. In many countries, moral rights like attribution and protection against distortion pass to heirs, allowing them to intervene if the work is misused. While U.S. law offers limited protection through VARA, artists with global audiences should plan with international standards in mind.

1. IP Duration After Death

In many regions, copyright protection extends well beyond the life of the artist, ensuring that heirs continue to reap the financial rewards of an artist's contributions.

In most major markets, including the United States, European Union, United Kingdom, Canada, and Japan, copyright protection lasts for the author's lifetime plus 70 years.

■ Artist Examples: Copyright Extension of Iconic Artists

- The masterpieces of Pablo Picasso (d. 1973) will remain shielded by copyright until 2043 in both the U.S. and the EU
- John Lennon's melodies (d. 1980) enjoy protection until 2050 in the U.S.

When the copyright period ends, these works move into the public domain, inviting anyone to share or utilize them freely.

2. Without an Estate Plan

When artists depart without a will or estate plan, their IP assets:

- Merge into their entire estate, divided according to the laws of intestacy (dying without a valid will)
- Face the risk of mismanagement or conflict among heirs
- Could be lost or underutilized if overlooked

● Prince's Estate Dispute (2016-Present)

Without a plan, even the most celebrated artists can leave behind legal chaos, and Prince's story shows what is at stake. The lack of a guiding estate plan stymied the distribution of his IP's worth, leading to a drawn-out struggle (Erskine, 2024).

>> Artist Takeaway: To avoid such turmoil, artists should define who inherits their intellectual property and outline how it is nurtured.

Hendrix Estate Battle

When iconic guitarist Jimi Hendrix died unexpectedly in 1970 at the age of 27, he left no will or estate plan. At the time, he was one of the most innovative and profitable musicians in the world, with significant intellectual property: recordings, unreleased music, merchandise potential, and performance rights.

Because there was no clear legal direction, his father, Al Hendrix, fought through years of court proceedings to gain control of the estate. After his father's death, further disputes erupted among other family members and business associates, leading to decades of legal battles, halted licensing deals, and brand confusion. Multiple lawsuits over trademarks, merchandise rights, and posthumous releases dragged on for over 30 years (Shenoy, 2017).

>> Artist Takeaway: Jimi Hendrix's legacy continues to generate millions, but much of that value was delayed, contested, or diverted because he didn't leave clear instructions about who should manage his work.

Designating IP Beneficiaries

To avoid future disputes, artists should decide who will inherit and manage their rights as soon as possible. A well-thought-out IP succession plan allows chosen heirs to receive royalties, licensing income, and ownership without complications.

1. Selecting IP Beneficiaries

Artists can tap various individuals or organizations to inherit and steward their intellectual property. Common beneficiaries include:

- Family – Spouses or children often inherit rights
- Charities – Royalties can be directed to nonprofits
- Businesses – Companies may inherit IP if they manage the work

■ Artist Example: Dr. Seuss's estate, overseen by Dr. Seuss Enterprises, continues to manage and monetize his beloved books, licensing deals, and adaptations. Thoughtful estate planning ensures his works remain profitable and culturally cherished (Dr. Seuss Enterprises, 2023).

2. Structuring Royalty Distribution

Artists who earn royalties from books, music, or licensing should clarify:

- How royalties will be distributed among heirs
- Whether to share royalties equally or reflect each heir's contributions
- Who will manage licensing agreements to secure ongoing income streams?

■ Artist Example: Paul McCartney reclaimed The Beatles' songs through U.S. copyright reversion laws after 56 years, highlighting the role of estate planning in adapting to changing IP laws (Paul McCartney Finally 'Gets Back' His Beatles Copyrights, 2018).

3. Preventing IP Disputes

Clear IP planning ensures your work passes smoothly to the next generation.

● The Case of Maurice Sendak

The visionary behind *Where the Wild Things Are* left a nebulous will, which led to a legal clash between his foundation and a library concerning his book collection and royalties (Blakemore, 2016).

>> Artist Takeaway: A clear IP and estate plan could have circumvented this challenge. Artists should document how their copyrights, royalties, and archives should be managed after death to avoid confusion, disputes, or mismanagement of their legacy.

Trusts and Wills for IP

Once you know who will receive your IP, the next step is setting up the legal structures that make those wishes enforceable.

1. Drafting an IP Will

A will directs who inherits copyrights, trademarks, and royalties.

- Thoroughly cataloging all copyrights, trademarks, and patents
- Naming a literary or artistic executor to oversee the IP
- Giving explicit instructions for licensing, sales, or donations of IP assets

Artist Example: Nipsey Hussle, celebrated for his music and business acumen, secured trademarks, music rights, and real estate before his passing in 2019, ensuring his family could maintain the "Marathon" brand legacy (Greenburg, 2020). (See Legacy Toolkit for the IP Will and Estate Planning Checklist.)

2. Creating an IP Trust

An IP trust acts as a legal vessel managing assets on behalf of beneficiaries. This structure ensures artworks are handled with professionalism, preventing financial mismanagement.

Advantages of an IP Trust

- Protects IP from potential misuse or unauthorized sales by heirs
- Oversees royalty payments over time
- Ensures consistent licensing strategies to foster ongoing revenue

Artist Example: Disney's family trust effectively manages his IP, ensuring continual profitability from films, characters, and trademarks (Allan Gray, 2023).

3. Appointing an IP Executor

The responsibilities of IP executors entrusted with overseeing assets posthumously include:

- Renewing copyrights and trademarks

- Negotiating licensing agreements
- Collecting and distributing royalty payments

▪ Artist Example: Bob Marley's estate maintains control over his music and brand, licensing his image and songs while safeguarding his artistic legacy (Cliff, 2015).

8.3 Selling & Transferring IP Rights

For some people, the right move isn't to hold onto IP, but to sell or transfer it as part of a broader legacy or financial plan. This section covers when to sell, how to structure agreements, and what to consider in global IP transactions.

When to Sell IP

Deciding when to sell your IP is a strategic move. Some choose to license their work for steady income, while others opt for a one-time sale to meet immediate financial goals. It all depends on your vision and what works best for your future.

1. Reasons to Sell IP

Quick Cash for New Goals - Selling your IP can bring in a lump sum, and is helpful if you:

- Need funds to launch a new project
- Want a clean exit from managing licenses
- Are planning your estate and want to simplify things for your heirs

The Market Is Hot:

- A songwriter might sell during a music rights boom
- A tech-innovator might cash in when a patent is in high demand

Less to Manage:

- Licensing your IP means handling contracts, tracking sales, and protecting your rights. Some artists sell to avoid the ongoing work

You're Done With It:

- If you don't see future use or interest in the work, selling might be the smartest financial move

2. Reasons to Keep IP

Earn Royalties Over Time:

- A novelist might keep earning from reprints, audiobooks, or film deals

Your Work Might Grow in Value:

- Art, music, and photography often become more valuable over time, sometimes even after your lifetime

Stay in Control:

- A filmmaker might lose creative input if they sell their screenplay rights

Pass It On:

- Think of how Elvis Presley's estate still earns from his music today

Sell vs. License Decision

Factor	Selling IP Rights
Payment Structure	One-time lump sum
Control Over Use	No control after sale
Financial Benefit	Immediate payout

Structuring IP Sales

When you choose to part with your IP, crafting a lucid and legally binding sales agreement becomes paramount to protecting your interests. (See the Legacy Toolkit for the IP Sales Agreement Template.)

Key Parts of Sales Agreement

A. Describing the IP – Articulate the IP you wish to transfer, covering the following:

- Copyrighted works such as visual arts, literary works, cinematic pieces, and musical compositions
- Trademarks that represent brand identities, graphical symbols, and catchphrases
- Patents that secure inventive concepts and distinctive methodologies

B. Payment & Valuation Terms – Clearly define these critical aspects:

- The total amount due, whether as a lump sum or through scheduled installments
- Any relevant royalty arrangements to ensure ongoing benefit
- Additional incentives based on the market success of the IP that demonstrates prominent demand

C. Transferring Rights & Ownership

- Specify if you are relinquishing complete ownership or retaining certain rights
- Clarify the nature of usage rights, whether they are exclusive or subject to particular conditions

D. Warranties & Representations – As the seller, you commit to ensuring:

- Your legitimate ownership of the IP
- The absence of claims from third parties on the IP
- No existing agreements that would conflict with this transaction

E. Indemnification & Dispute Resolution

- Highlight the protective measures each party has in place
- Detail the path for resolving misunderstandings, whether through mediation or legal proceedings

International IP Transfers

Navigating the sale of IP across borders can feel like treading through a maze where each turn reveals different national laws, tax complexities, and enforcement obstacles.

1. Global IP Laws & Jurisdiction

Each country has a unique set of IP laws that determine how long protections last and how they must be maintained:

- Copyrights typically last for decades, often extending beyond the artist's lifetime
- Trademarks require regular renewal and ongoing commercial use
- Patents may be enforceable internationally with the right treaties and filings in place
- Contracts help define ownership, duration, and applicable law, ensuring IP rights are respected across borders

Example: The Madrid Protocol streamlines international trademark registration, allowing artists and brands to file one application that covers multiple countries.

2. Tax & Financial Implications

Cross-border IP transactions often involve complex tax and financial considerations:

- Royalties may be subject to taxation, though international treaties can help reduce or eliminate double taxation

- High-value IP transfers may result in capital gains tax liabilities, depending on the jurisdictions involved

Example: Creators in the U.S. who venture into the European market might encounter tax liabilities from both American and EU authorities, unless a treaty eases the financial burden.

3. Enforcing IP After Sale

Once an IP asset changes hands, guaranteeing adherence to contractual obligations internationally can be quite intricate.

- Some jurisdictions may lack strong frameworks to uphold copyright protections
- Trademark holders should maintain vigilance against global infringement

Example: Disney's Global IP Protection

Bob Dylan's $300M IP Sale

Bob Dylan's sale of his full catalog, including 600+ songs, marked a major shift in music IP valuation (Sisario, 2020). It transferred complete copyright ownership, giving Universal control over licensing, royalties, and global distribution. For Dylan, it provided an immediate lump sum but meant giving up long-term earnings and control. Universal, now the sole rights holder, can leverage the catalog worldwide, shaping how future generations experience his music.

>> Artist Takeaway: Selling your intellectual property can bring significant upfront capital, but it means giving up future royalties and control. Deals like Dylan's show how corporations view IP as long-term assets. For artists, such sales demand careful contracts covering licensing, royalties, and global rights.

How you choose to manage your work, through retention, licensing, or sale, should align with your financial needs, long-term vision, and legacy planning.

The Art of IP Ownership

Owning your creativity shapes your future. Every IP decision influences how your work is seen, valued, and preserved. The tools you've explored — copyrights, trademarks, patents, licensing, infringement protections, and estate planning — are more than legal steps: they're foundations for control, value, and legacy.

Managing your IP means protecting your voice and making your artistry work for you. While technology, law, and culture will keep evolving, the core idea stays the same: know your rights, claim your space, and create on your terms.

Own it. Protect it. Thrive.

Your creativity is your greatest gift and an asset that is uniquely yours. In a world abundant with ideas, those who protect theirs will be able to leverage them and own their brand. The preceding chapters have provided you with the tools, knowledge, and strategies to ensure that your art and vision remain yours. Intellectual property is not just a legal concept; it is the bedrock of a successful career and vital to turning your passion into enduring success. Reading ***The Creative Shield*** has initiated your journey toward the success you deserve.

However, knowledge without action is just potential without results. Now you must step forward with confidence and claim your space in the world with a brand that stands alone and strong against imitation and infringement. Trademark it, copyright it, license it, and, most importantly, believe in its worth. The future belongs to those who protect what they create.

Legacy Toolkit

IP Estate Checklist

IP Sales Agreement

Early Career

- Start copyright registration
- Trademark your artist name
- Get comfortable with contracts

Growth Phase

- Expand your trademark portfolio
- Diversify through licensing & merch
- Enforce your rights against infringers

Mid-Career

- Build a portfolio of copyrights
- Explore design patents
- Innovate with new media like NFTs

Legacy Planning

- Plan your business succession
- Assign or bequeath IP rights
- Consider a trust or IP holding company

Extra Toolkit

IP Quiz Pack

Obscure IP Facts

Fair Use/Public Domain Links

DIY Copyright Notice

IP Self Audit Quiz

Copyright Reversion Guide

Next Steps

You've learned the tools, now it's time to put your protection into motion.

1. Lock in Your Identity

    ▢ Define your name, slogan, or visual brand elements.
    ▢ Search for similar names or logos already in use.
    ▢ Complete the Claiming Your Creative Identity Workbook.

2. Register & Protect Your Work

    ▢ Register key works with the U.S. Copyright Office.
    ▢ Use the Filing Checklist and Walkthrough Video.
    ▢ Consider trademarking your name, logo, or slogan.

3. Organize Your IP Portfolio

    ▢ Store all registrations, contracts, and licenses digitally.
    ▢ Use the IP Portfolio Tracker Template.
    ▢ Back up records and set reminders for renewals.

4. Get Clear on Contracts

    ▢ Review or update contracts with clients or collaborators.
    ▢ Understand the difference between work-for-hire and licensing.
    ▢ Customize the Work-for-Hire Template or License Comparison Table.

5. Expand Internationally (If Needed)

    ▢ Research local IP laws for international licensing.
    ▢ Register IP in key regions or through WIPO.

6. Defend & Enforce Your Rights

    ▢ Know how to issue a cease-and-desist if needed.
    ▢ Save the DMCA Template or use the Cease-and-Desist Generator.
    ▢ Monitor your brand and work online.

7. Protect Your Creative Legacy

    ▢ Decide who will manage your IP if needed.
    ▢ Complete the Estate Planning Worksheet for Artists.
    ▢ Talk with a trusted person about your creative wishes.

Reflections

References

Aaker, D. A. (1996). *Building strong brands.* The Free Press.

Abloh, V. (2017). *OFF-WHITE trademark registration.* United States Patent and Trademark Office.

Allan Gray Proprietary Limited. (2023). *Disney: The value of strong intellectual property in a changing world.* Allan Gray.

Art Girl Army. (2017). *Collective archive.* https://artgirlarmy.com

Associated Press v. Fairey, No. 09 Civ. 1123 (S.D.N.Y. 2011). Associated Press Settles Copyright Lawsuit Against Obama 'Hope' Artist. Wired. https://www.wired.com/2011/01/hope-image-flap/

ATP Journal. (2022, August 31). The Etsy copyright infringement problem: Is Etsy safe for artists? ATP Journal. https://journal.atp.art/etsy-copyright-infringement/

Basquiat Estate. (2022). *Basquiat trademarks and licensing.* https://basquiat.com

Blakemore, E. (2016, November 8). Legal dispute over Maurice Sendak's epic book collection gets wild. Smithsonian Magazine. https://www.smithsonianmag.com/smart-news/

Bright Tunes Music Corp. v. Harrisongs Music, 420 F. Supp. 177 (S.D.N.Y. 1976).

Budds, D. (2015, September 18). How Pantone became the definitive language of color. Fast Company.
https://www.fastcompany.com/3050240/how-pantone-became-the-definitive-language-of-color

Buza, J. (2022, December). Not everything ironic is eligible for trademark registration: The case of Off-White. Tramatm.
https://www.tramatm.com/blog/category/fashion/not-everything-ironic-is-eligible-for-trademark-registration-the-case-of-off

Caves, R. E. (2000). *Creative industries: Contracts between art and commerce.* Harvard University Press.

Cheng, A. (2023). Monster Energy's trademark battles in gaming. Game Industry Report.

Cliff, A. (2015, February 21). Everybody, stop putting Bob Marley's face on stuff now. The FADER. https://www.thefader.com/2015/02/21/bob-marley-estate-wins-image-use-case

Cohen v. G&M Realty L.P., 320 F. Supp. 3d 421 (E.D.N.Y. 2018). https://casetext.com/case/cohen-v-gm-realty-lp-2

Cowan, Liebowitz & Latman, P.C. (2023, February 16). *MetaBirkins NFTs found to infringe Hermès' trademark rights.*

Congdon, L. (2021). *Art, Inc.: The Essential Guide for Building Your Career as an Artist.* Chronicle Books.

Copyright Act of 1976, 17 U.S.C. §§ 101–810.

Cornell Copyright Information Center. (2023). *Copyright basics and public domain overview.* https://copyright.cornell.edu

Day, K. (2022). *Licensing agreement – Wall art example. Kellie Day Art.* https://kelliedayart.com/wp-content/uploads

Delaney, B. (2016, September 26). *'You could disappear into it': Anish Kapoor on his exclusive rights to the 'blackest black'. The Guardian.* https://www.theguardian.com/artanddesign

Dr. Seuss Enterprises. (2023). *Licensing and collaborations.* https://www.drseussenterprises.com/licensing-and-collaborations

Economic Times. (2016, December 30). Disney wins 'Cars' copyright suit in China, to receive $194,600 as compensation. https://economictimes.indiatimes.com/magazines/panache/disney-wins-cars-copyright-suit-in-china-to-receive-194600-as-compensation

Electronic Frontier Foundation. (2023). *Fighting patent trolls in the creative industries.* https://www.eff.org

Erskine, M. (2024, January 17). *The battle for Prince's estate: Unending conflict, legal drama, and lessons for family business. Forbes.* https://www.forbes.com/sites/matthewerskine

Ethereum Foundation. (2021). EIP-2981: *NFT royalty standard*. https://eips.ethereum.org/EIPS/eip-2981

European Union Intellectual Property Office (EUIPO). (2022). *Full Colour Black Ltd. v. Pest Control Office Ltd.*, R1246/2021-5. https://euipo.europa.eu/copla/trademark/data/017981629/download

Flood, A. (2013, October 30). Stephen King: 'I have outlived most of my critics'. The Guardian. https://www.theguardian.com/books/2013/oct/30/stephen-king-interview-doctor-sleep

Florida, R. (2019). *The rise of the creative class*. Basic Books.

Getty Images v. Stability AI, No. 23-cv-00135 (D. Del. 2023). BakerHostetler. https://www.bakerlaw.com/getty-images-v-stability-ai

Gladwell, M. (2000). *The tipping point: How little things can make a big difference*. Little, Brown and Company.

Godin, S. (2003). *Purple cow: Transform your business by being remarkable*. Portfolio.

Graham v. Prince, No. 15-cv-10160 (S.D.N.Y. 2024). https://www.courthousenews.com/artist-richard-prince-to-pay-hundreds-of-thousands-of-dollars-to-photographers-in-new-portraits-copyright-suits/

Gray v. Perry, No. 2:15-cv-05642 (C.D. Cal. Mar. 16, 2020).

Greenburg, Z. O. (2020, December 15). Inside Nipsey Hussle's blueprint to become a real estate mogul. *Forbes*. https://www.forbes.com/sites/zackomalleygreenburg/2019/02/20/nipsey-hussle-opportunity-zone-real-estate-mogul-blueprint/

Griffin v. Sheeran, No. 1:17-cv-05221 (S.D.N.Y. 2023)

Heath, C., & Heath, D. (2007). *Made to stick: Why some ideas survive and others die*. Random House.

Herald Sun. (2023, November 11). Chinese retail juggernaut sold design stolen from Torquay artist.

Hermès International v. Rothschild, No. 22-cv-384 (S.D.N.Y. 2023). https://www.skadden.com/insights/publications/2023/02/jury-finds-that-metabirkin-nfts-infringed-hermes-trademark-rights

Hobbs, T. (2021). Taylor Swift's masters: A case study on artist rights and brand control. *Billboard Magazine.*

Holt, D. B. (2004). *How brands become icons: The principles of cultural branding.* Harvard Business Review Press.

In re Estate of Andy Warhol, 629 N.Y.S.2d 621 (Surr. Ct. 1995). https://www.ifar.org/case_summary.php?docid=1313777348

Kapferer, J. N. (2012). *The new strategic brand management: Advanced insights and strategic thinking.* Kogan Page.

Keller, K. L. (1993). Conceptualizing, measuring, and managing customer-based brand equity. *Journal of Marketing, 57*(1), 1–22. https://doi.org/10.1177/002224299305700101

Kinsella, E. (2018, October 25). The first AI-generated portrait ever sold at auction shatters expectations, fetching $432,500—43 times its estimate. *Artnet News.* https://news.artnet.com/market/first-ever-artificial-intelligence-portrait-painting-sells-at-christies-1379902

Lange, A. (2020, September 29). When life looks like a Wes Anderson movie. *The New York Times.* https://www.nytimes.com/2020/09/29/movies/wes-anderson-design-buildings.html

LEGO A/S v. ZURU Inc., No. 3:18-cv-2045(AWT), 2019 WL 4643718 (D. Conn. July 8, 2019), aff'd, 2020 WL 3046200 (Fed. Cir. June 8, 2020).

Lehmann Maupin, LLC v. Yoo, No. 157743/2018 (N.Y. Sup. Ct. 2018).

Lessig, L. (2004). *Free culture: How big media uses technology and the law to lock down culture and control creativity.* Penguin Books.

Louboutin v. Yves Saint Laurent, 696 F.3d 206 (2d Cir. 2012).

Louis Vuitton Malletier S.A. v. Louis Vuiton Dak, 123 F. Supp. 3d 456 (S.D.N.Y. 2023).

Matal v. Tam, 582 U.S. 218 (2017).

Meyer v. Conan Doyle Estate Ltd., 2020 WL 5590240 (S.D.N.Y. 2020).

Mitchell Studio. (2021). *Tyler Mitchell visual style & branding.* https://tylermitchell.co

Murakami Studio. (2020). *Trademark portfolio and branding strategies.* [Removed URL – brand site only]

Naruto v. Slater, 888 F.3d 418 (9th Cir. 2018). https://law.justia.com/cases/federal/appellate-courts/ca9/16-15469/16-15469-2018-04-23.html

New York City Department of Consumer and Worker Protection. (2023). *Freelance Isn't Free Act.* https://www.nyc.gov/assets/dca/downloads/pdf/workers/Freelance-Isnt-Free-Law-English.pdf

Nolan Heimann. (2021). *Celebrity inventors, patents & innovation.* https://www.nolanheimann.com

Northeastern University. (2025, July 9). *Can Scarlett Johansson sue OpenAI over its voice assistant? Northeastern intellectual property law experts weigh in.* https://news.northeastern.edu/2025/07/09/johansson-openai-sky

Nouns DAO. (2024). *A generative NFT token project on Ethereum.* https://nouns.wtf

One Little Independent Records. (n.d.). *Official website.*

Paul McCartney finally 'gets back' his Beatles copyrights. (2018, October 29). *Pace Intellectual Property, Sports & Entertainment Law Forum.* https://pipself.blogs.pace.edu/2018/10/29/paul-mccartney-finally-gets-back-his-beatles-copyrights/

Peterson, J. (2021, November 30). *Hanna-Barbera character STAR: A lesson in descriptive trademarks.* That's a Trademark. https://www.thatsatrademark.com/blog/hanna-barbera-star

Ritson, M. (2019, October 7). Beyoncé vs Blue Ivy: A lesson in trademark law and brand power. *Marketing Week.* https://www.marketingweek.com/beyonce-blue-ivy-trademark-law/

Ryzik, M. (2019, July 5). How the Michael Jackson estate made $2 billion after his death. *The New York Times.* https://www.nytimes.com/2019/07/05/arts/music/michael-jackson-estate.html

Saint Heron. (2021). *Creative licensing and brand protection.* [Removed link – brand-only site]

Schwarz, H. (2021, August 25). Bob Ross's family wants you to know the joy of painting wasn't always joyful. *The Washington Post.* https://www.washingtonpost.com/arts-entertainment/2021/08/25/bob-ross-documentary-family-response/

Shenoy, S. (2017, September 18). The tangled legacy of Jimi Hendrix. *NPR.* https://www.npr.org/sections/therecord/2017/09/18/551543915/the-tangled-legacy-of-jimi-hendrix

Sherman, E. (2011). Shepard Fairey and AP settle lawsuit over Obama 'Hope' poster. *The Hollywood Reporter.* https://hollywoodreporter.com

Sisario, B. (2020, December 7). Bob Dylan sells his songwriting catalog in blockbuster deal. *The New York Times.* https://www.nytimes.com/2020/12/07/arts/music/bob-dylan-universal-songwriting.html

Sisario, B. (2023, May 4). Ed Sheeran wins copyright lawsuit over 'Thinking Out Loud'. *The New York Times.* https://www.nytimes.com/2023/05/04/arts/music/ed-sheeran-copyright-verdict.html

Stanford University Libraries. (2023). *Fair use and trademark basics.* https://fairuse.stanford.edu

Telfar Global. (2021). *Trademark and trade dress registration.* [Removed link – brand-only site]

Tiffany & Co. (n.d.). Trademarks & copyrights. https://www.tiffany.com/policy/trademarks-copyrights/

TinEye. (2023). *Tracking image use online.*

Tintin fan club wins legal fight with Hergé heirs over image rights. (2015, June 9). *The Guardian*. https://www.theguardian.com/world/2015/jun/09/tintin-author-herge-rights-moulinsart-casterman

Tolkien Estate. (2023). *Frequently asked questions and links.* https://www.tolkienestate.com/frequently-asked-questions-and-links/

United Nations Educational, Scientific and Cultural Organization. (1971). *Universal Copyright Convention as revised at Paris on 24 July 1971. UNESCO.*

U.S. Code. (n.d.). 17 U.S.C. § 203 – Termination of transfers and licenses granted by the author. Cornell Law School. https://www.law.cornell.edu/uscode/text/17/203

U.S. Copyright Office. (2018). *Music Modernization Act: A summary of key provisions.* https://www.copyright.gov/music-modernization/

U.S. Copyright Office. (n.d.). *The Digital Millennium Copyright Act.* https://www.copyright.gov/dmca/

U.S. Copyright Office. (2023, February 21). Re: Zarya of the Dawn (Registration # VAu001480196). https://www.copyright.gov/docs/zarya-of-the-dawn.pdf

U.S. Copyright Office. (2023c). *Work-for-hire and licensing basics.* https://www.copyright.gov

U.S. Copyright Office. (2025). *Copyright and Artificial Intelligence: Part II – Copyrightability.* https://www.copyright.gov/ai/part2/

U.S. Department of the Treasury & Government of Canada. (1980). Convention between the United States of America and Canada with respect to taxes on income and on capital. https://www.irs.gov/pub/irs-trty/canada.pdf

U.S. Trademark Application Serial No. 90449849, "DOJA CAT," filed January 5, 2021. United States Patent and Trademark Office.

U.S. Trademark Database. (2023). https://tmsearch.uspto.gov

U.S. Trademark Registration No. 6304203, "BRENT FAIYAZ," registered March 30, 2021. United States Patent and Trademark Office.

United States Congress. (1990). *Visual Artists Rights Act of 1990*, 17 U.S.C. § 106A. https://www.congress.gov/bill/101st-congress/house-bill/2690

United States Copyright Office. (2023). https://www.copyright.gov

United States Patent and Trademark Office. (2019). U.S. Trademark Serial No. 88409370 (Billie Eilish Blóhsh).

United States Patent and Trademark Office. (2025, February 13). Office action outgoing for U.S. Trademark Application Serial No. 98408937. U.S. Department of Commerce.

United States Patent and Trademark Office. (n.d.). Trademark status and document retrieval: Serial No. 85446652 (OFWGKTA). U.S. Department of Commerce. https://tsdr.uspto.gov

United States Patent and Trademark Office. (n.d.). Trademark status and document retrieval: Serial No. 88893188 (VERZUZ). U.S. Department of Commerce. https://tsdr.uspto.gov

VPM. (2019, August 28). What Missy Elliott did for Afrofuturism. https://www.vpm.org/watch/2019-08-28/what-missy-elliott-did-for-afrofuturism

Wiley, K. (n.d.). *Kehinde Wiley Studio*.

Williams v. Gaye, 895 F.3d 1106 (9th Cir. 2018). https://casetext.com/case/williams-v-gaye-4

Wischhover, C. (2017, September 8). Rihanna's Fenty Beauty line is going where no other beauty brand has gone before. *Vox*. https://www.vox.com/the-goods/2017/9/8/16274780/fenty-beauty-rihanna-launch-diversity

World Intellectual Property Organization. (1979). *Berne Convention for the Protection of Literary and Artistic Works (Paris Act, 1971) as amended on September 28, 1979*. https://www.wipo.int/treaties/en/ip/berne/

World Intellectual Property Organization. (1996). *Madrid Protocol: Protocol relating to the Madrid Agreement concerning the international registration of marks.* https://www.wipo.int/madrid/en/

World Trade Organization. (1994). *Agreement on Trade-Related Aspects of Intellectual Property Rights (TRIPS).* https://www.wto.org/english/docs_e/legal_e/27-trips.pdf

Young Turks. (2020). *FKA twigs performance and visual assets.* [Removed link – brand-only site]

Appendix A

Exclusive vs. Non-Exclusive License

PARTIES: This Licensing Agreement ("Agreement") is made and entered into on [Date], by and between:

Licensor: [Name of Licensor] Licensee: [Name of Licensee]

1. GRANT OF LICENSE:

- Exclusive License: Licensor grants Licensee the exclusive right to use, distribute, reproduce, and display the licensed work ([describe the work]) in the agreed-upon market/territory for the duration of this Agreement. No other parties, including the Licensor, may use the work during this period.
- Non-Exclusive License: Licensor grants Licensee a non-exclusive right to use, distribute, reproduce, and display the licensed work ([describe the work]), but retains the right to license the work to other third parties.

2. TERM AND TERMINATION:

- The Agreement shall commence on [Start Date] and continue until [End Date], unless terminated earlier by either party in accordance with the terms herein.
- Either party may terminate this Agreement with [Notice Period] written notice if the other party breaches any material term of this Agreement.

3. COMPENSATION & ROYALTIES:

- Exclusive License: Licensee agrees to pay Licensor a one-time fee of [$Amount] OR a royalty rate of [X%] on all revenue generated from the licensed work.

- Non-Exclusive License: Licensee agrees to pay Licensor a licensing fee of [$Amount] OR a lower royalty rate of [X%] due to the non-exclusive nature of this Agreement.

4. RIGHTS & RESTRICTIONS:

- Exclusive License: Licensee may sublicense, modify, or create derivative works only with Licensor's consent (or as otherwise agreed upon).
- Non-Exclusive License: Licensee may use the work but may not sublicense or modify it without prior written approval from Licensor.

5. INDEMNIFICATION: Both parties agree to indemnify and hold each other harmless from any claims, damages, or liabilities arising from the use of the licensed work.

6. GOVERNING LAW: This Agreement shall be governed by and construed in accordance with the laws of [Jurisdiction].

7. SIGNATURES: By signing below, both parties agree to the terms and conditions set forth in this Agreement.

Licensor: Signature: ______________________________

Printed Name: ______________________________

Date: ______________________________

Licensee: Signature: ______________________________

Printed Name: ______________________________

Date: ______________________________

Appendix B

YouTube Copyright Claim

YouTube

Hi Creator,

After a manual review, a copyright owner has claimed some material in your video.

Your video is live and the visibility settings you selected remain applied to it. But it is now either being monetized by the copyright owner, or they have chosen to receive analytics about it.

This is not a copyright strike. This claim does not affect your account status.

Video title:
Copyrighted content:
Claimed by:

Next steps

- If there are no problems, you don't need to take any action and you don't need to delete your video.
- If something went wrong and the copyright owner or our system made a mistake, we have a dispute process. Only use it if you're confident you have the rights to use all the content in your video. Learn more
- You can also remove the claimed content using Studio's editing tools.

View options

Need copyright-safe songs?
When choosing music for your next video, you can avoid copyright-related issues by picking a song from the YouTube Audio Library. We're adding new tracks all the time!

- The YouTube Team

Help center • Email options

Appendix C

Essential IP Terms

IP Basics

Copyright – The exclusive legal right to reproduce, distribute, perform, or display an original work of authorship (e.g., art, music, writing). Automatically exists upon creation but offers stronger legal protection if registered

Public Domain – Creative works not protected by copyright and freely available for public use, typically because copyright has expired or the creator voluntarily released them

Trademark – A word, logo, slogan, color, or design that distinguishes your brand identity from others in the marketplace. Used to prevent consumer confusion

Patent – A government-granted right to exclude others from making, using, or selling a new invention or process for a limited time (typically 20 years)

Trade Dress – The visual appearance of a product or its packaging (e.g., shape, color, layout) that signifies its source and may be protected under trademark law

Intellectual Property (IP) – A general term for creations of the mind (art, music, inventions, designs) protected by copyright, trademark, or patent law

Moral Rights – The right of artists to claim authorship and to object to derogatory treatment of their work, even if they don't own the copyright (more recognized outside the U.S.)

Trade Secrets - Private business info (like formulas or processes) that stays protected by keeping it confidential, no registration needed, just strong safeguards

Copyright & Registration

Fair Use – A legal doctrine allowing limited use of copyrighted work without permission for purposes like commentary, criticism, parody, or education

Cease-and-Desist Letter – A formal notice sent to an infringer demanding they stop unauthorized use of protected work or face legal action

Work-for-Hire – A contract where the hiring party, not the artist, becomes the legal author and copyright holder of the created work

Derivative Work – A new, original work based on a copyrighted piece (e.g., remix, sequel, or adaptation), which requires permission from the original copyright owner

Infringement – Unauthorized use of copyrighted, patented, or trademarked material, subject to penalties or lawsuits

DMCA Takedown Notice – A formal request submitted under the Digital Millennium Copyright Act to remove infringing content from online platforms

Statutory Damages – Pre-set monetary damages awarded by courts in infringement cases if the copyright was registered before the violation occurred

Registration Certificate – An official record from the Copyright Office or USPTO confirming your IP ownership and legal rights

Trademarks & Brand Identity

Fanciful Mark – An invented or made-up word (e.g., Kodak) that is inherently distinctive and offers the strongest trademark protection

Arbitrary Mark – A real word used in an unrelated context (e.g., Apple for computers) that is highly protectable under trademark law

Suggestive Mark – A mark that implies qualities or features of a product, requiring consumer imagination (e.g., Netflix)

Descriptive Mark – A mark that directly describes a characteristic or function of a product (e.g., "Cold and Creamy" for ice cream); only protectable with secondary meaning

Generic Term – A common word for a product or service that cannot be trademarked (e.g., "Bread" for a bakery)

Secondary Meaning – When a descriptive mark becomes uniquely associated with a particular source through long-term use and recognition

USPTO – The United States Patent and Trademark Office, where trademarks and patents are filed and registered

Madrid Protocol – An international treaty that allows creators to register a trademark in multiple countries with one application

Contracts, Licensing & Deal Structures

License – A legal agreement granting someone permission to use your intellectual property under specific terms, while you retain ownership

Exclusive License – A license that gives one person or entity the sole rights to use your work, often for a higher fee

Non-Exclusive License – A license that allows multiple parties to use your work simultaneously

Royalty – A payment (usually a percentage of sales or profits) made to the creator or IP owner for the use of their work

Minimum Guarantee – A guaranteed minimum payment agreed upon in a licensing deal, even if royalties fall short

Kill Fee – A contractual payment owed to an artist if the client cancels a commissioned project before completion

Indemnification Clause - A contract term where one party agrees to compensate the other for certain legal claims or losses

Usage Restrictions - Specific limits in a contract on how, where, or for how long a work can be used by the licensee

Term & Termination Clause - Part of a contract that defines the length of the agreement and how it can be ended

Digital, Tech & Legacy Planning

NFT (Non-Fungible Token) - A unique digital asset, registered on a blockchain, representing ownership of art, music, or collectibles

Smart Contract - Code embedded in NFTs or blockchain systems that automatically enforces licensing terms, such as royalties on resale

Metadata - Embedded information in digital files (e.g., authorship, copyright, creation date) used for IP tracking and protection

Digital Watermark - A visible or invisible mark on digital images used to identify ownership and deter unauthorized use

AI-Generated Content - Creative works made with the help of artificial intelligence; current law may not recognize copyright unless significant human authorship is involved

IP Portfolio - The collective body of copyrights, trademarks, and patents owned by a creator or business, often treated as financial assets

Estate Planning for IP - The process of managing and transferring IP rights upon an artist's death, including wills, trusts, and beneficiary designations

IP Sales Agreement - A contract that outlines the full transfer of intellectual property ownership from one party to another, often for a lump sum

Author

Zamani Thomas is an intellectual property attorney with over two decades of experience advising Fortune 500 companies, entrepreneurs, and award-winning artists on how to protect and profit from their work. Known for his clear, accessible approach to legal education, he bridges the gap between creativity and the law, helping clients navigate copyrights, trademarks, licensing, and brand protection.

He is the founder of The Creative Docket, a multidisciplinary platform dedicated to empowering artists through law, storytelling, and creative exploration. While legal knowledge remains its core thread, the platform also features fiction, resources, and tools designed to inspire and support artists in the digital age.

The Creative Shield: The Artist's Guide to Copyrights, Trademarks & Brand Monetization is the first installment in a three-part series that helps artists navigate the evolving landscape of content, commerce, and code.

www.ingramcontent.com/pod-product-compliance
Lightning Source LLC
LaVergne TN
LVHW022218200926
848481LV00006B/2018
* 9 7 8 1 0 6 9 4 1 4 4 4 1 *